MY KUMAON

Jim Corbett was a pioneer in many respects—
a hunter par excellence with over a dozen
man-eaters (thought to have taken more than
1,500 lives) to his name and a committed
conservationist who helped establish India's
first national park (later named after him).
Corbett was also a consummate storyteller whose
adventurous and perceptive tales have not only
entertained and captivated a whole generation of
readers, but also opened their eyes to the cause
of the environment. His books—*Man-Eaters
of Kumaon* (1944), *The Man-Eating Leopard of
Rudraprayag* (1948), *My India* (1952), *Jungle Lore*
(1953), *The Temple Tiger and More Man-Eaters of
Kumaon* (1954), and *Tree Tops* (1955)—continue
to remain bestsellers even today.

MY *Uncollected Writings*
KUMAON
JIM CORBETT

OXFORD
UNIVERSITY PRESS

OXFORD
UNIVERSITY PRESS

Oxford University Press is a department of the University of Oxford.
It furthers the University's objective of excellence in research, scholarship,
and education by publishing worldwide. Oxford is a registered trademark of
Oxford University Press in the UK and in certain other countries

Published in India by
Oxford University Press
YMCA Library Building, 1, Jai Singh Road, New Delhi 110001, India

Typeset in 11/16 Dante MT Std
by Excellent Laser Typesetters, Pitampura, Delhi 110 034
Printed in India by G.H. Prints Pvt. Ltd, New Delhi 110 020

Photographs taken from OUP Archives, Oxford, UK;
reprinted by permission of the Secretary to the
Delegates of Oxford University Press.

Contents

SECTION ONE
THE UNPUBLISHED CORBETT

Publisher's Note

In 2012, Oxford University Press celebrates a hundred years of publishing in India. This is a time to look back as well as move forward. Over the years, the Press has nurtured close relationships with its authors, of which Jim Corbett is, perhaps, the best known. British hunter, naturalist, and a conservationist, Corbett is famous for slaying a large number of man-eating tigers and leopards in the Kumaon region of northern India. Frequently called upon by the government of the United Provinces during the 1920s and the 1930s, Corbett is known to have slain nineteen tigers and fourteen leopards. Some of these man-eaters were given names—such as the Champawat Tiger, the Leopard of Rudraprayag, the Tigers of Chowgarh, and the Panar Leopard—all of which have become the stuff of legend. His successes earned him both gratitude and fame, and the people of Kumaon often describe him as a saint.

Corbett was encouraged to write about his hunting experiences by Roy E. Hawkins, manager of the Indian Branch of Oxford University Press, and a personal friend. *Man-Eaters of Kumaon* (1944),

The Man-Eating Leopard of Rudraprayag (1948), *My India* (1952), *Jungle Lore* (1953), *The Temple Tiger and More Man-Eaters of Kumaon* (1954), and *Tree Tops* (1955) have had commercial and popular success over the years, and continue to be bestsellers even today. In 1978, Roy E. Hawkins brought out a collection of unpublished stories by Corbett in a book titled *Jim Corbett's India*. All these books—written in a racy style full of suspense and detail—are popular with children, naturalists, preservationists, and even hunters, and are in keeping with India's attempts to conserve its dwindling number of tigers.

OUP India's centenary has provided us with an opportunity to go back to the archives—both in India and in the UK—to search for the evolution both of Corbett's books and his relationship with the Press. During the search, we found letters, notes, reviews, and articles highlighting Corbett's engagement with the times in which he lived, his complete empathy with the people of Kumaon, and his great understanding of tigers. This volume presents Corbett's unpublished essays, personal diary entries, articles written for newspapers and gazettes by his contemporaries, and letters between Corbett and his editors (especially Roy E. Hawkins)—all culled from the archives of Oxford University Press. They showcase the man and his love for the people of Kumaon who accepted 'a total stranger at his face value', and where he spent his 'happiest days'.

As with all findings that go back fifty years and more, sources for some of the articles have been lost. Thus, while the name of the publication in which Lord Hailey's 'A Life Well Lived' first appeared remains untraced, the names of the authors of 'The Artlessness of his Art' and 'The Man Revealed: Corbett in his Writings' are also missing. However, since the material contained in them was so interesting, we have chosen to include them in this volume.

This addition to the Corbett corpus of titles is being brought out during our centenary year. Besides being a tribute to the author and

the long-lasting value of our publishing, this title also commemo-
rates the enduring relationship between the Press and Jim Corbett
who has been one of its best-selling writers since *Man-Eaters of
Kumaon* was first published in 1944.

Jim Corbett

A Chronology

1862: Jim Corbett's parents move to Naini Tal, India, where Corbett's father, Christopher Corbett, is appointed the postmaster of the town.

1875: The Corbetts move to a newly-built two-storey house below Alma, the second lowest of the hills around Naini Tal. In winter, the family moves to the foothills of Naini Tal to live in a cottage called 'Arundel' at Kaladhungi, in Choti Haldwani (or Corbett's village).

Birth of Jim (Edward James) Corbett, on 25 July, in Naini Tal, to Christopher Corbett (widower, with three children) and Mary Jane Corbett (widow, with three children), the eighth of thirteen children.

1881: Death of Corbett's father, Christopher. Mary Corbett decides to sell their house in Alma and move across the valley to a spot 1,000 feet higher—on the safer Ayarpatta Hill. The new home is named 'Gurney House'.

1883:   Corbett is gifted his first firearm: a double-barrelled muzzle-loading shotgun, the right barrel of which was unusable. He is also gifted a limited supply of powder and shot. Jim is just eight-and-a-half years old. His first targets are birds which he begins to hunt with his dog, Magog.

1885:   Corbett is loaned a .450 Martini rifle from the Naini Tal armoury, with a set of sights especially calibrated for him, and a never-ending supply of bullets. The only stipulation is that he looks after the gun, keeps it clean, and returns the empty shell cases, so that the brass from which they are made can be recycled.

1886:   Corbett kills his first leopard. He is eleven years old.

1894:   Corbett quits school, and gets a job with the Bengal and North-Western Railway (the BNWR) as fuel inspector in Manakpur, Punjab.

1895:   Corbett becomes trans-shipment inspector with BNWR, and is sent to Mokameh Ghat in Bihar. He later becomes a contractor for the trans-shipment of goods across the Ganges at Mokameh Ghat. He works at Mokameh Ghat for almost twenty years.

1907:   Corbett agrees to go after the Champawat Tiger which is known to have killed 438 humans. The government had offered huge rewards to kill this beast and had assigned *shikaris* (hunters) and Gurkhas from the army to hunt it down but none had succeeded. Corbett agrees on two conditions: all hunters are to be called back from the jungles, and cancellation of the reward. For Corbett, killing a man-eater is a social obligation; he does not want the jungles filled with trigger-happy hunters.

1910:   Corbett shoots the Muktesar Tiger and the Panar Leopard; he also handles 5,500 tons of goods in a single day at Mokameh Ghat, a record.

1915:   Corbett buys 221 acres of land around Choti Haldwani for Rs 15,000 from Guman Singh Barua. The *chaupal* (meeting place), Moti House (built for his friend Moti Singh), and the Corbett wall (7.2 km wall built to protect the village from wild animals)—all built by Corbett—still stand.

1920:   Corbett settles down in Naini Tal to look after his mother, his sister Maggie, and his stepsister Mary Doyle.

Corbett becomes vice-chairman of the Naini Tal Municipal Board. He remained a participating member till 1944.

1922:   Along with Percy Wyndham (commissioner, Kumaon Division for twelve years), Corbett buys a share in a coffee estate on the slopes of Mount Kilimanjaro, Kenya. He begins to go there for three months each year.

1925:   Corbett kills the man-eating leopard of Rudraprayag. The leopard had claimed 114 victims.

1928:   Corbett obtains a Bell & Howell 16 mm movie camera, a gift from Lord Strathcona.

1933:   Corbett builds his outdoor studio, which he guards jealously from intrusions by hunters and poachers.

1935:   Together with F.W. Champion (an English forester, who worked in British India and became famous in the 1920s as the first wildlife photographer and conservationist), Corbett plays a key role in establishing India's first national park in the Kumaon Hills. It is named Hailey National Park after Lord Malcom Hailey (Governor of the United Provinces, 1928–34). In 1957, it is renamed Corbett National Park in honour of Jim Corbett.

Self-publishes the little known *Jungle Stories* which later becomes the basis for *Man-Eaters of Kumaon.*

1940–2: Serves on the District's Soldier's Board; recruits 1,400 men for a Pioneer Corps.

1943: Corbett fights in the humid jungles of Burma, and falls victim to typhus fever. He is forced to leave the army, and spends months recovering in a wheelchair.

1944: Corbett is commissioned as lieutenant colonel, and put in charge of training men for warfare in the jungles of Burma. Here he catches malaria, and is ill for a long time.

Man-Eaters of Kumaon is published by OUP India. Corbett is seventy years old.

1947: The Corbetts leave for Kenya. 'Gurney House', Corbett's Naini Tal home, is sold for Rs 55,000 to Sharda Prasad Varma. Corbett divides his 221 acres of land into forty lots, and gifts them to the villagers. Also, he continues to pay land revenue tax on behalf of the villagers till his death in 1955.

1948: *The Man-Eating Leopard of Rudraprayag* is published by OUP.

1952: *My India* is published by OUP.

1953: *Jungle Lore* is published by OUP.

1954: *The Temple Tiger and More Man-Eaters of Kumaon* is published by OUP.

1955: *Tree Tops* is published by OUP.

Death of Jim Corbett, on 19 April, in Nyeri, Kenya.

1957: Hailey National Park named Corbett National Park.

1965: The government buys Corbett's winter home in Choti Haldwani from one Chiranji Lal Shah (to whom Corbett had given it in lieu of the Rs 14,000 he owed him).

1967: The government converts Corbett's winter home 'Arundel' into the Jim Corbett Museum.

1968:   A New Annamese race of tigers—the *Panthera tigris corbetti*—is named after Jim Corbett.

1976:   The Government of India issues a stamp to commemorate Jim Corbett's birth centenary.

'How I Came to Write ...'

... On arrival at Government House that evening, the pleasure my hostess expressed, when in answer to her question I told her I had made a start, so shamed me that I, there and then, resolved to write up some of my experiences, even if no one ever took the trouble to read them. I have frequently been asked how many notebooks I have filled with my experiences, and I do not think I have always been believed when I have answered that I do not possess a notebook, and that I have never made a note in my life. If one uses one's senses as [they] were intended to be used, there is no need to make notes for everything that one sees and hears. [It is all] photographed in one's memory and is there for all time. [The] writing up, therefore, of stories I selected was not difficult ...

From my great collection of photographs, I selected eight. When I had copied them, I took the stories to a friend who had a small hand printing press. He had never before printed books, but being a good friend, he undertook the job. His stock type was, however, so limited that he was only able to print one page at a time and, after my sister and I had made what corrections were necessary, he printed off a hundred copies. The type was then broken up and set for the next page. In this way, he took four months to print the book which we called 'Jungle Stories'. I retained one copy and then I started distributing the other copies to friends. But owing to demands for additional copies for relatives in other parts of the world, I was only able to give seventy-five friends copies. These copies drifted from hand to hand until the majority had been read to death …

A concerted demand was then made for me publishing my stories in regular book form. But before I was able to make a start, Hitler started out on his land collection tour. Anticipating this tour by one week, I cut ten years off my age, took an application for a war job to Command Head Quarters. After I had been on service [for] two years, I contracted tick typhus. I entered hospital weighing twelve [and a] half stone. When I was discharged three months later, I weighed seven stone. I was told I would have to be content …

—Extract from an undated early telegram by Jim Corbett

A Life Well Lived

An Introduction to Jim Corbett

Jim Corbett is so modest and unassuming a man that he must have hesitated long before he committed himself to authorship. I doubt, indeed, if he could ever have been persuaded to it, but for the hope that the royalties on his book might aid the Hostel for blinded Indian soldiers. He would, perhaps, have had even greater qualms if he had foreseen that the world might be curious to learn more about himself than his book has revealed. For his own world has been that of Kumaon, its hills and jungles, and the simple folk who inhabit them. Certainly I myself, drawing on the memories of my friendship with him, am unable to see him otherwise than against that background, and if I write more about that than about him, it is because I know he would prefer me to do so.

He belongs to one of those English families which have made their domicile in India. I recall that he had a stepsister, much older than himself, who, in her childhood, had been among the beleaguered garrison of Agra in the dark days of the Mutiny of 1857. Men of these families, born and educated in India, have often an understanding of Indian ways of life which is not given to those whose sojourn is only for their term of office. A property, which he inherited in the Kumaon Hills in Naini Tal, has given him independence to follow the life to which his own instincts have inclined. He was educated at Naini Tal, and there has his home, but he spends the winter months in a small estate at Kaladhungi at the foot of the hills. He is unmarried, but all his life has had the devoted companionship of his sister, Margaret, who has made his ways her own.

In the War of 1914–18, Jim took to France a labour corps from the Kumaon Hills, and many tales are told of the unquestioning faith with which the hill-men followed his leadership in the unfamiliar world to which he led them. If I am right, his first visit to England was paid when he was on leave from France. At the end of the War, he returned, with the rank of Major, to resume his life in Kumaon. During the recent War, the Army again sought his services, and he helped to train in jungle warfare the troops who were to take part in the campaign in Burma. It was a young man's job, and Jim was no longer a young man; but he carried it through, until he fell victim to tick fever in the steamy lands of central India.

There, in short, is the history of his life; but the story would be incomplete without its setting. First, then, of Naini Tal. Picture a lake some 6,000 feet above the plains, set deep in a circlet of hills, clad with cypress and fir. Legend relates that the first Europeans who visited it, soon after the Gurkhas were driven out of Kumaon in 1815, resolved to keep to themselves the secret of its existence, so delectable did it seem to them. But, that was not to be, and around the shores of the lake there has grown up a hill station to which the Government of the United Provinces has, for many years, resorted during the summer heat of the plains. There is a popular belief—and events have given it some warrant—that the goddess of the lake has avenged herself for this official intrusion on her privacy by exacting the yearly toll of a victim in her waters.

But, the interests which have filled Jim Corbett's life have not been in Naini Tal so much as in the country which surrounds it. At no great distance to the south lie the jungles and ravines of the Bhabar foothills, haunt of game, both great and small. Further to the south-east is the low-lying and swampy Terai, with its leagues of tall and almost impenetrable grasses, where malaria saps the strength of man and the tiger is king. Northwards of the lake, the hills mount steadily up to merge in the majestic massif of the Himalayas. From the top of Cheena, chief of Naini's encircling hills, you may see the rising sun light up the ice-clad pinnacles of Trisul and Nanda Devi; in the further distance stands Kamet, the highest of the Himalayan peaks yet conquered by man, with the shrine of Badrinath at its foot, whither pilgrims flock yearly to worship the source of the holy Ganges.

Surroundings such as these were rich in opportunity for the life of sport, for which nature seemed to have designed Jim Corbett. Even in his later years, he retains the spare form, the untiring muscles and insensibility to hardship or hunger which long days and nights in the jungles and on the hills demand. And he has rare gifts of eye and hand. To those who use the twelve-bore gun for small game, there is something uncanny in his performance with his light twenty-eight bore; his handling of the rifle for big game recalls some of the storied feats of the Wild West gunmen; and how often have I not looked with envy on his mastery over the fighting fish of the Kumaon rivers.

Nevertheless, I do not think that it is the pursuit of beast or bird or fish which have ever held the chief attraction for him. His real interest has been in the wildlife of the jungles and the hills, and from boyhood he has trained himself to observe and study it. The belling of the deer, the chattering of the monkeys, the calling of birds—each of these has its own meaning for him. And, as the years have passed, the desire to observe and record the ways of wildlife has more and more absorbed him. He has become a confirmed addict of the cine-camera. There are difficulties in its use in the Indian jungles, for their denizens cling to the deep shade, and seldom offer those suspiciously clear shots which Hollywood seems able to produce to order. Nor has India had the great game reserves such as abound in Africa, where lions are always ready to oblige by posing for the camera.

For the tiger, in particular, he has developed a feeling which almost amounts to tenderness. I have more than once been with him when villagers have come to complain of the ravages of a marauder. And let me add, that they have shown a fitting sense of our respective values. The Governor of a Province of nearly fifty million people was entitled to some respect; but their allegiance was clearly for Jim Corbett, for it was he who could relieve them of the Terror that walked by night. They knew how long and often how dangerous might be the task of one who must pit himself against the cunning of the confirmed man-eater. But Jim would weigh the indictment. The lord of the jungle must be given his rights. The killing of cattle and goats was not a capital offense; wilful homicide must be proved. But once proved, he would not stay his hand until the malefactor had been executed, and those simple and kindly folk could return to their deserted hamlets, and once more till the hillside fields from which they win their scanty living. The tiger was entitled to his due, but man came first.

Lord Hailey, Former Governor of the Punjab and
the United Provinces of India

SECTION ONE

The Unpublished Corbett

The Nightjar's Egg

I have often wondered while reading a book about what impelled the author to write it. Was the idea born with him, and grew up as he grew, getting stronger each day until, eventually, he simply had to write the book? Or, did he one night, while brushing his hair before going to bed, say to himself 'Tomorrow I shall write a book' and, on the morrow of his resolve, go out and buy a fountain pen or a typewriter and reams of foolscap paper and sit himself down before a comfortable fire and, selecting two of his friends for the role of hero and heroine, follow them through many scenes and over much ground until, eventually, the hero went off to the wars, or was led to the altar.

We who read books, and here I do not refer to the classics or books on science and art, but to the ordinary books we receive from book clubs, or that we buy off a bookstall, are never told by the authors how these books came to be written. So, to leave no doubt in your mind, I am going to tell you how a book that I have inflicted on you came to be written.

The impulse to write the book was not born with me, nor did I while brushing my hair, suddenly and for no reason at all, determine to write the book. But I had a very determined friend and, in a weak moment, I promised this friend that I would put some of my experiences on paper, in book form. Having made the promise, I had to keep it. The prospect of writing a book was terrifying and, the more I thought about it, the more terrified I became. Friends appealed to were not helpful: 'Oh, just sit down and write.' Sitting down was easy enough, but writing was my difficulty for I had no idea how to begin. 'Once upon a time' was not appropriate, for I had no fairy tales to tell. And then, the comforting thought came to me that it mattered little how I began, how many chapters there were, and how many words in each chapter; for no one except the person at whose bidding I was writing the book, would take the trouble to read it. Having come so far along the rough track that all who undertake an unfamiliar task must follow, I found, to my great relief, that the track ahead of me was smooth and comparatively easy and, best of all, very pleasant. All I had to do was to select a few experiences over a long period of years, and put down on paper a word description of those mind photographs.

In a Reader's Union book a short while ago, there was a soliloquy by a lone voyager as to why scenes witnessed years previously, even as far back as childhood, remained fixed in one's memory while the scenes witnessed the day before could only be recalled—if recalled at all—with an effort. He came to the conclusion that this was due to our mind being more receptive when we are young, than it is as we grow older. With this conclusion I do not agree. When we are young, our horizons are limited, and the few things that interest us are indelibly etched on our memories. As we grow older, our horizons enlarge, and an increasing number of things interest us; but the impressions are not etched in for the simple reason that we have neither the time nor the inclination to make as detailed and clear etchings as we made when we were young. The mind is not at fault for distorted and faint impressions for, I believe that our minds—up to a point—remain receptive throughout our lives, and the fault of making bad and faint impressions instead of good clear-cut ones is not due to an enlarged horizon, but due to a lack of concentration and interest.

From my very earliest childhood, everything in nature has interested me intensely, with the result that all I have seen and all the experiences I have met with over a very long period of years have been indelibly etched on my memory and the scenes of yesterday are as clear as the scenes of half a century and more ago.

A tiger had called during the previous night and yesterday; towards evening, my sister and I had gone out to see where the tiger had come from, whether it had remained in our vicinity and, if not, where it had gone to. The jungle in which the tiger had called is about a quarter of a mile wide, and is bounded on the east and west by the wide open and stony beds of two streams, dry in this season of the year and raging torrents when the monsoon rains fall on the hills which start a mile away. We had proceeded half a mile up the west bed looking for the tiger's pug marks on the footpaths and game tracks that cross it when, as we were walking over a bed of stones, I asked my sister who was walking on my right, to stop. We had our backs to the sun which was near setting, and I had seen a shadow which I recognized as being cast by a nightjar which had apparently risen from the stones just in front of her. My sister had been looking to the left at the time, and had not seen the shadow and, on her asking me what had attracted my attention, I told her not to move forward for, if she did so, she would probably put her foot on the eggs of the nightjar which had just risen. When nightjars sit out in the open at this season of the year, they only do so because they are sitting on eggs. After looking carefully, we saw a single egg; there was no attempt at a nest: just the one single egg laid among the stones on a small patch of sand a few inches square.

We found where the tiger had entered the jungle the previous evening. It had killed and eaten a small chital (spotted deer) and had left the jungle early that morning. On the way home, we discussed the possibility of my taking a cinema picture of the nightjar and her egg. In one of the stories in the book I have inflicted on you, I have mentioned how difficult it is to see a nightjar on the ground. I have also mentioned the bird's eggs, and it occurred to me that it would be nice to have a cinema picture of the bird we had found and of her egg. So, this morning I loaded my camera with a Kodachrome film and, accompanied by one of my men, set out to take the picture. I had not taken any special note of where the bird was in that big expanse of stony ground, but this did not matter for I knew I should recognize the spot when I came near it. Thirty yards from where I expected the bird to be, I stopped, took the camera out of its case, wound it up, set the lens at F8, and set the range at 15 feet. I then took the man to the little bit of high ground that I had measured with my eye as being 15 feet from the bird; from here the bird was visible. It was impossible to make the man believe that the brown-coloured object with a faint yellow line on it was a bird; so, lying down to steady the camera, I exposed a few feet and keeping the camera running, signalled to the man to go forward, and took the bird as it rose off its egg. I then took a close up of the egg and return-ing to the high ground sent the man away, intending to take the bird as she returned to the egg. But she was suspicious, and after flying round my head several times, she flew away. Afraid that the hot sun would addle the egg if exposed for any length of time, I got to my feet and, rejoining the man, returned home.

Part of the events I have narrated took place yesterday, and part took place today. And I am confident that if you were to question me about them tomorrow, or ten years hence, I would from memory be able to retell the story of the nightjar, word for word, as I have told it above. And this cannot be attributed to my mind being young and receptive; but it can be attributed to my having taken an interest in the scene which is now indelibly etched into my memory.

Reverting to the book, and my relief on realizing that possibly only one person would trouble to read it, I turned over the pages in my memory and, selecting a few scenes covering a long period of years, started to put a description of them down on paper. I am not a writer of books, and I cannot hope that I have succeeded in describing those scenes to you as I saw them. For this, do not blame my memory, for the scenes are as clear and as finely etched today as when I witnessed them, but blame my lack of words, and be assured that I have tried to get you to follow me step by step through those scenes, and let you see through my eyes what I saw, adding not a single line to the etching, and leaving out only those details that would unnecessarily harrow your feelings. If I succeed in taking you with me to the last page of the book, I am content.

'One of Us'

'Sorry.' 'So sorry.' 'Oh, I
am so sorry.' For the third
time, the tall lad walking
behind me had stepped on my heel,
pulling off my thin rubber-soled shoe.
He was one of a party of twenty-five lads
I had taken into the jungle the previous
day, and I had noticed as we left camp that
morning that he had manoeuvred to walk
immediately behind me. Lacing up my shoe for
the third time, I told the tall lad that it would be less
embarrassing for both of us if he walked in front of
me. 'Oh please, not in front,' he said, 'but may I walk
by your side?' The game track was too narrow for two
to walk abreast, so while he kept to the track, I walked in
the jungle by his side.
At the first bit

of open ground we came to, I called a halt and made the party sit down in a semi-circle facing me, for it was quite apparent that the nervousness of the tall lad was infecting his companions. I will now leave the lads sitting in the jungle, while I explain the reason for their being there.

On the outbreak of Hitler's War, I was appointed Deputy Military Vice President, District Soldiers Boards, and posted to the Meerut Command which embraced the five districts of Dehra Dun, Muzaffarnagar, Meerut, Bulandsher, and Aligarh. These districts, with a population of sixteen million, were very proud of the fact that, for over a hundred years, they had provided the bulk of the recruits for the Indian Army. Throughout the Command, there was hardly a village that did not have Army pensioners, or men serving with the armed forces in the Middle East, Singapore, or Hong Kong. My duties were many and varied and, in particular, were to look after the interests of some hundreds of pensioners, and be a father and mother to the wives and families of men on active service.

I do not think there is a more interesting post in the Indian Army or one that brings a man into closer or more intimate touch with rural India, than that of Deputy Military Vice President, District Soldiers Boards, during wartime. The only qualifications needed for the post are a love for the people, the ability to speak their language, and an iron constitution. A volume could be written of my experiences during the two years I held that post, covering 30,000 miles by road and visiting many villages where no other white man had ever set foot. This, however, is not a record of the little I did and the lot I left undone while associated with the poor and hospitable people who welcomed me wherever I went and gave me of their best, and two experiences are all that space will permit of my relating.

I was motoring at midday from Moradabad to Meerut. It was the month of May, and the heat rising off the road could be seen and smelt. Birds and beasts were sheltering from the sun, and the only living thing in sight was a figure in the distance going in the same direction as I was. Presently, this figure resolved itself into a bare-headed and a barefooted man in a saffron-coloured robe, with a stick over one shoulder to which was attached a small bundle, and carrying a beggar's bowl. Stopping the car on reaching the man, I opened the door and said, 'Come inside brother. On such a day it is permitted for a pilgrim on his way to Badrinath to cool the soles of his feet for a little while.' He was a man of about my own age and height but three stone heavier, his robe was clinging to his body, and little rivers of sweat were running down his face and onto his great expanse of chest. 'Were it my first pilgrimage, I would not accept your offer, but being my third no merit will be lost if, as you say, I cool the soles of my feet for a little while.'

Extracting a big *roomal* from his bundle, he mopped his head and face and, shaking the dust off his feet, climbed heavily into the car and sat down beside me with a sigh of contentment.

'I cannot pay more than one rupee for travelling in your car,' he said, 'so put me down when you consider I have had a rupee's ride.'

While talking, he opened the knots in a corner of his roomal, and taking there from a silver rupee, he offered it to me.

'Is this all you have?' I asked.

'Yes.' He answered, 'It is all I have and you must judge how far it will carry me and perchance that may be to the next roadside well, where I can spend the night.'

'Have you no friend on this road who will give you food and shelter for the night?'

'Yes, I have such a friend, but he is three days' walk from here.'

He went on to tell me that his friend was the custodian of a small temple on the left bank of the Ganges, 30 miles further along the road on which we were travelling.

'Make yourself comfortable,' I said, 'and don't keep putting your head outside the car to see where the next roadside well is, for I will take you as far as your friend's temple, not for the rupee you have offered me but for the pleasure of your company.'

'I know now who you are,' he said. 'You are he who gives people a ride in his car and demands no payment. But those who told me about you were wrong in saying you were a Sahib, for you are no Sahib, you are one of us, a Rajput.'

Flattered that my Hindustani was sufficiently fluent for a man who travelled extensively to have mistaken me for a co-religionist, I did not immediately undeceive him, and finding in me a good listener, he told me of his life both before and after becoming a sadhu. In the course of this recital, he mentioned a village. Now, it so happened that a riot had taken place in that village a few days previously in which several Army pensioners had been beaten up, and that very morning I had attended a meeting called by the Collector of Moradabad to enquire into the cause of the riot. The War at that time was at a critical stage and enemy agents were active, inflaming communal feelings which were resulting in riots, and the slowing down of recruiting. It was suspected that this subversive movement was organized by a handful of men, but their names were not known. Part of my duties was to counter enemy propaganda and help in recruiting, and my friend sitting beside me was now telling me about the organization and its leaders for his home, when he was not on the road, was in the village in which this last riot had taken place. It was because of the riot that he had decided to go on his third pilgrimage to Badrinath, for being a sadhu and a man of peace, he did not want to get mixed up with communal troubles.

Near a small whitewashed temple buried deep in a mango grove, I stopped the car for the sadhu to alight. As I closed the door on him, he asked my name. 'So that I can remember it in my prayers.' And when I told him, he looked steadily at me, nodding his head as he did so and then, in a very hurt voice, he said, 'You probably have very good reasons for trying to hide your identity, but why insult an old man by telling him a lie?'

With these words the sadhu left me, taking my good wishes with him for I had enjoyed his company, and he had left with me three names the knowledge of which restored communal peace in many a village in the Meerut Command.

The father of a man serving in the Middle East had written to him complaining of the behaviour of his wife. The son took the letter to his Commanding Officer, with a request for compassionate leave. The Army was hard-pressed at the time, and leave could not be granted. So the letter was sent to me, with a request to look into the matter. Seventy miles on a tarmac road, 10 miles along a cart track, and 2 miles over ploughed fields brought me to a small village sheltering under a giant banyan tree. Fifty or more peafowl roosting in the tree through the heat of the day resented my presence, and warned the village of my approach. I had no difficulty in finding the writer of the letter, who was an Army pensioner with three medals won in wars on the North-west Frontier of India. The medals, with their frayed and faded ribbons, were produced for my inspection with great pride, and with even greater pride I was told that his only son was serving with his old regiment in Misr (Egypt). After I had replenished the medal ribbons—I always carried a pocketful for the purpose—I asked the old man if he had heard recently from his son. 'No,' he said, 'I have not heard from my son recently, but I am expecting him home any day now.' 'But,' I said, 'you have just told me that he is on active service and you, an old soldier, know that on active service leave can only be granted in a case of life and death. Here there is no such case for you have told me that your son has no children, and that his wife is well.' 'True,' he said, 'my son's wife is well, but it is in connection with her that I have written to my son to come home.' He then went on to tell me, what I already knew, for I had his letter in my pocket, that his daughter-in-law was giving him a lot of anxiety, and that he feared she would bring disgrace on his son and on his family.

'If there is no purdah in your house, can I see your son's wife?' I asked. 'Yes,' he answered, 'you can see her, for there is no purdah for you.'

I was sitting on a string bed in the shade of the banyan tree, with the old man sitting on the ground near me. He now got up, and going to a neat little mud-built house with a tiled roof, called out, 'Moonia, there is one here who would speak with you.' Presently, a girl appeared at the door and, after a little hesitation, accompanied the old man to where I was sitting. On coming up to me, the girl said, 'What have you to say to me?' And, without waiting for an answer, continued. 'Has *sasur* (father-in-law) been complaining to you about me as he tells me he has complained to my man?' And then, in a flood of words, she said, 'What have I done to bring disgrace on my man? Am I a widow that I must sit all day in my house with a chaddar over my head, and never go out to see any of my friends? And now, not content with complaining to my man, sasur has been complaining to you, or why should you want to speak with me?' 'No, no,' I hastened to assure her, for her lips were trembling and she was on the point of tears. 'I have not been listening to any complaints about you, but being in the village and hearing that your man was on service in Misr, I thought that maybe you would like to send a message to him through me, for his Commanding Officer is a friend of mine.'

An hour later, I left the village. In my notebook was a message for Moonia's husband telling him that all was well with her, and that the red cow had calved and was giving 2 seers of milk, half of which was being converted into ghee against his return. From the old man I extracted a promise that, in return for a request for his son's name to be put on the list of men next due for leave to India, he would withdraw his objection to Moonia visiting her friends, and would send no further complaints about her to his son. These matters settled to everyone's satisfaction, and to the accompaniment of the screaming peacocks overhead, I was presented with the refreshments that Moonia and her mother-in-law had prepared for me. In India, the lavish hospitality of a Raja or a Nawab can be declined without giving any offence, but not so the hospitality of a poor man. He gives of his best, and he gives it in the only manner known to him, and to decline the hard-boiled egg that has been shelled for you with fingers recently released from a plough, or to decline the cup of tea stirred with a stick picked up off the ground would cause grievous hurt to sensitive feelings, for it would be interpreted as meaning that the food offered was not considered good enough.

With slight variations, Moonia's case was repeated in nearly every village throughout the Meerut Command, for tens of thousands of men were on active service, and nowhere does the writ of Mother Grundy run stronger than it does in rural India. Happily, during the two years I served in that command, I did not meet with a single case where the presence of a man on active service was needed to safeguard the honour of his home.

And then came Pearl Harbor, followed by an air attack on Rangoon. No provision had been made to maintain law and order, or to carry on the day to day work of a city in the face of an enemy attack and the mass exodus of its civil servants. When, therefore, Ibbotson (Sir William) returned to India from a flying visit to Rangoon, he ordered the immediate formation of 10 Pioneer Battalions to deal with similar situations should they arise from air attacks on Indian cities. I was offered the command of the 10 battalions, but as this meant an office chair in Delhi, I declined the post and offered, instead, to raise and command a battalion of hill men. My offer was accepted, and while I was raising the battalion at Bhim Tal on the Maharaja of Jind's estate (which he had very kindly placed at my disposal), I contracted a very virulent form of tick typhus said to have been introduced into India by the Boer prisoners during the South African war. I entered the Ramsay Hospital in Naini Tal weighing 12 stone and, after three months of expert treatment and devoted nursing, left it weighing 8 stone. I was invalided out of the Army with the prospect of spending the rest of my days in an armchair, but as this prospect did not appeal to me, I concentrated all the energy that had been left to me in an effort to get well, ably assisted by my sister Maggie. Six months later, I appeared before a very sympathetic medical board, and the next day was back in the Army.

On this occasion, I was appointed Lecturer on Jungle Lore, and attached to the Central Command whose headquarters were in Agra. This command embraced the major portion of Central and Northern India, and in it were two training divisions, 300 miles apart, and an independent brigade. The 14th division under the command of General Courts, and the independent brigade under the command of Brigadier Davies were based, respectively, in Chhindwara and Budni in the Central Provinces, and the 39th under the command of General Moore was based in Saharanpur in the United Provinces. The combined strength of these two divisions and the independent brigade varied between 50,000 and 70,000 according to the number of recruits entering, and the trained troops being drafted out of them. Reinforcements were urgently needed in the field, and I do not think that a more devoted band of men ever worked harder to provide those reinforcements than the commanders and the staffs of the three units I have mentioned. Nor do I think that a finer lot of Indian and British lads—for they were little more—has ever been called upon to fight with less training a more fanatical enemy under harder conditions. I had the privilege of being associated with these lads from 1942 to the end of the War, and though during that period I never met a single lad who was *pining* to get to grips with the Japs, I met many thousands who, without having any illusions about the fighting qualities of the enemy, were nevertheless willing to fight him on the ground of his choice. No praise is too high for these lads, many of whom gave their all, only to find a grave in the Burma jungles.

As I was the first and the last man ever to be appointed Lecturer on Jungle Lore, there were no chapters and verses in the Army Bible, known as King's Regulations, to help me in my work, and as no one could tell me what that work was, I was left entirely to my own resources. For three months I travelled between the two divisions and the brigade, spending all my nights on the road and my days in lecturing to drafts on the eve of their departure for the front. And then, General Scoones, fresh back from the fighting in Burma, took over the Central Command, and summoned me to headquarters. It is amusing now to recall that visit of twelve years ago. I made an early start from my hotel, and walked the 4 miles to Command Headquarters where I was met by a very harassed Major who greeted me with the words, 'Thank heaven you are punctual.' I had been many times to that headquarters where no one was ever in a hurry, and where uniforms were only donned on very special occasions. Now all was changed. Telephone bells were ringing, staff of all ranks was hurrying in and out of doorways, and along passages and verandas, *and all were in uniform.*

Shepherding me into his room and giving me a chair, the Major expressed the hope that I was prepared for my interview. He said there was a tiger now in the big room at the end of the veranda, and that, if I did not want my head bitten off, it would be advisable to run through any notes I had brought with me. I had brought no notes for I never make any so, while I smoked, the Major worked furiously to resolve some figures he was having difficulty with. I had nearly finished my cigarette when a Staff Captain put his head in at the door, and said briefly, 'GOC wants to see you Sir,' and then hurried off on some other errand. The Major, for all his 14 stone, lacked nothing in agility, and the message had hardly been delivered before he was through the door and striding down the veranda. Presently, I heard him hurrying back, so I met him at the door. 'Come with me,' he said grimly, and though I have long legs, he beat me by a yard to the door at the end of the long veranda. At the door, he only paused long enough to announce me, and then hurried off on some errand of his own.

Here too, in the big room, all had changed. The walls, on which had hung some steel engravings, were now draped with enormous war maps, liberally adorned with coloured flags. The table that had occupied one corner of the room was gone, and gone too was the attractive and very efficient typist who used to work at it. The big green baize covered table in the centre of the room, that had always been so tidy and on which a bowl of flowers always stood, was now littered with papers and, sitting at the table in an old and faded jungle green battle dress, was the 'tiger'. 'A big-hearted gentleman…' In the year 1928, the first cage in the tiger house at the London Zoo was occupied by a tiglon—half a tiger and half a lion—one of the finest animals I have ever seen. If you stood in front of the cage, as I did on many occasions, the tiglon would look with a steady gaze right through to your bones and out the other side. When the sitter at the table bade me come in and take the central of three chairs—'where I can see you for I like to look at people I am talking to'—I had the same feeling that I had when standing in front of the tiglon's cage. There was interest but no hostility in the steady gaze across the green baize table, and I knew my head was in no danger of being bitten off.

The interview lasted for over an hour, and was wholly satisfactory. My difficulties in dashing from one part of India to another in an attempt to instruct too many people in too short a time was appreciated and, to avoid further loss of time, it was arranged that I should establish jungle camps in the areas of the three units to which I was attached. The selection of sites for these camps would be left to me, and to them would be sent parties of twenty-five men of all ranks selected by their battalion commanders. These parties would remain with me for a fortnight and, on return to their respective units, would pass on what they had learnt from me. The conditions under which the men would live in camp would simulate, as far as possible, the conditions prevailing in Burma. No weapons of any kind, batmen, cooks, or strong drinks would be allowed in the camps, and as it was my intention to establish these camps in jungles in which there was big game of all kinds, I would be held responsible for the well-being and the safety of the men entrusted to me. Numbers of men were being lost and dying of starvation in the Burma jungles, and it would be part of my duties to train my charges not to get lost and, when necessary, to live in the jungles. Here, I was faced with a difficulty for though I knew every edible flower, fruit, vegetable, and root in the Indian jungles, I was ignorant of the flora of Burma. It was, therefore, arranged that I should fly forthwith to Burma and, armed with a letter of introduction to General Slim who at that time was commanding the 14th Army; see as much as I could of the Burma jungles. Thanks to the kindness of General Slim, I spent a very pleasant and a very instructive month on the operational front and, on my return to India, I had a second interview with General Scoones before setting off to establish my first jungle camp.

On a Sunday morning, towards the end of the winter, I met my first party of twenty-five British lads, at a brigade headquarters in the 39th Division. They had been selected by their respective unit commanders and all were volunteers, for I had made it quite clear that I would have no pressed men in my camps. In a jeep driven by a bearded Sikh, I piloted the two lorries containing the party, our kit, and rations for a fortnight, along forest roads for 40 miles, and then for 10 miles along fire-tracks that had not previously been used for motor traffic. Starting after breakfast and clearing the tracks of fallen trees and big stones, our progress was slow, and we arrived at 5 p.m. near the site I had selected for our camp. This site was at the edge of a dense forest on the right bank of a little stream, and 300 yards from the fire-track. When the jeep and lorries had left us to return to headquarters, we carried the kit and rations to camp, and spent the remaining daylight hours in collecting firewood, drawing water from the stream, and in clearing away the dead wood and dry leaves from the ground on which the lads were to sleep. When this had been done, and sanitary trenches dug, there was no time to cook a dinner. So we sat around the camp fire and brewed tea, and made a meal off tinned rations.

It had been a strenuous day for all, and when heads began to nod, I banked up the fire and, leaving the lads to lay down their valises on the ground we had cleared, went back to the fire-track where I had left my kit. Here, under a box tree that was in bloom and filling the night air with scent, I laid down my valise and, within a few minutes, was fast asleep. The moon was on the wane and, just as it was rising, I was awakened by hearing a tiger calling, half a mile up the fire-track. Again and again the tiger called, each time a little nearer. The tree under which I was lying was some 10 feet below, and about 20 yards from the fire-track. At the nearest point of the track to me, a great slab of rock jutted out from the side of the hill. Presently, on this rock I saw the tiger silhouetted against the sky. For a long minute the tiger stood on the rock, and then it jumped down onto a game track which, starting from the fire-track on the far side of the rock, ran down to the stream and up the 20 feet high bank, on the far side. At the top of the bank, the game track divided, one arm going through the camp where the lads were sleeping and the other arm skirting round and above the camp. On climbing the bank and seeing the glowing embers of the camp fire, and the recumbent figures near it, I knew the tiger would take the upper track. Even so, I listened anxiously until I heard a sambhar bell once, and again on the shoulder of the hill on the far side of the camp.

Next morning, after rolling up the valises, burying the food tins that had been emptied the previous night, and generally tidying up the camp, I set out with the party of lads with the avowed object of having a walk through the jungles before breakfast, but actually to try and find the kill which I suspected the tiger had been making for when I heard it calling the previous night. None of the lads mentioned having heard the tiger so I said nothing about it, my intention being to lead them to the kill, if I could find it, and then bring them back over the tiger's tracks to show them how close to them it had passed the previous night. For, I had seen from the tiger's pug marks that it had done exactly as I had expected it to do.

This then was the position when, after having had my heel trodden on for the third time, I left the party of twenty-five lads sitting in a clearing in the jungle, while I explained the reason for their being there.

From My Jungle Camp

I like, best of all, to hold my classes in the jungle. It is so much easier, and more natural to discourse about jungle matters when a multitude of nesting birds are pouring out their sweetest songs, and Paradise Flycatchers are flitting through the trees and, may be, a karkar or sambhar is calling in the distance, than it is to lecture in crowded camps to the accompaniment of lorries changing gear, and jeeps and motorcycles roaring past.

Men of all ranks, hailing from Land's End to John-O-Groats and of all castes and creeds between Cape Comorin and Peshawar, attend my classes.

I am styled Lecturer on Jungle Lore but it would be more correct to style me Demonstrator, for, whenever and wherever possible,

I try and teach by actual demonstration. The lad who has climbed a tree to secure an articular fruit—seen for the first time—or who has delved 4 feet into the ground to unearth a particular tuber will never again need to be told that the fruit and tuber are edible, or where and how to find them. Nor, after he has once heard it at close quarters, will he ever again mistake the deep-throated growl of a tiger for thunder, or the belling of a sambhar for a motor horn; and not only that, he will also know what these sounds indicate, and what importance to attach to them.

Travelling as I do from jungle camp to jungle camp, I meet with many amusing experiences. One day, as I approached a camp to collect my class, I saw a gibbon high up in a Samal (silk cotton) tree, eating the big fleshy flowers which bloom in March. I stood and watched the animal for some time, and was interested to see how it floated from branch to branch as lightly as a feather, and without any apparent effort. My class of thirty officers was waiting for me in the camp, and I took it to a secluded spot in the jungle and sat down on a rock with my back to the camp, while the class sat in a semi-circle facing me. I had been talking for some time on different subjects when I noticed that the attention of the lad on the extreme right of the semi-circle had been attracted by something behind me; presently I noticed that others were interested in the same object. What this object was, I could not think, until I suddenly remembered the gibbon. Without turning my head or interrupting my talk, I waited until the converging eyes of the class apprized me that the gibbon had come up close behind me. I had no idea what the animal's intentions were and, as I felt her brush against me, I raised my left arm and very deliberately she took her seat in my lap, putting her long arms round my neck, while I put my arm round her shoulders. For the next half hour, the gibbon sat without sound or movement in my lap and, before concluding my talk, I apologized for her presence and said her only reason for attending the class was to satisfy herself that I told no lies about our ancestral home. I learnt, later, that the unit I was with had brought the gibbon back from Assam, and had given her the freedom of the jungles.

On another occasion, after I had assured my class that no danger need be apprehended from tigers and other animals provided a few jungle rules were strictly adhered to, I took my class numbering seventeen into a nearby jungle to look for tracks, edible fruit and roots, and so on. We had only proceeded a short distance when a tigress who objected very strongly to our approaching her kill— possibly a sambhar—shooed us out of the jungle. My companions, only one of whom had ever seen a tiger, behaved like veterans and, following out instructions, retreated foot by foot and we came out of the adventure, admittedly a little hot under the collar, but without a single scratch.

The subjects I deal with are many and varied and include:

1. Attitude of wildlife towards man, with special reference to so-called dangerous game
2. How to look for, and where to find, edible fruit, flowers, plants, barks, and roots
3. How to make fire from jungle materials, and methods of cooking when utensils are not available
4. Fruit and herbs that can be used to cure ailments resulting from irregular diet, exposure, chills, etc.
5. How to distinguish between the bites of poisonous and non-poisonous snakes, and treatment for the former
6. How to avoid leech bites
7. How to remove ticks to avoid sores and irritation resulting from their bites
8. Treatment for scorpion stings

9. How to treat jungle itch
10. How to procure water from certain plants, and how to get clean water from contaminated streams and buffalo wallows
11. How to make birdlime and nooses
12. How to make booby traps
13. How to make calls to imitate jungle sounds
14. How to distinguish between animal and man-made sounds, how to stalk, take cover, and so on

I encourage my classes to ask questions, and the questions I am asked cover a very wide field. A few days ago, a lad, whose home I imagine is in Inverness, asked me if I had ever been stalked and, if so, what my reactions had been. He little knew what a host of memories his question aroused: memories dating back to 1907 when my first encounter with a man-eater nearly cost me my life and, extending up to 1939 when, for a whole week, I was stalked by a man-eating tiger.

I will tell you the story of that first encounter in the hope that it will help you to avoid making a mistake similar to the one I made, and which nearly cost me my life. All of us are not given the opportunity of learning by experience, but we can benefit by the experience of others.

I was out on that occasion after a tigress that had many hundreds of human kills to her credit. I had done a certain amount of tiger shooting, but this was the first man-eater I had ever had anything to do with. She was, in fact, the first man-eater that had ever been known in that area, so there was no one to whom I could appeal to for advice in dealing with her.

For six days, I searched for the tigress in the dense jungles from which she had driven away the entire human population and, on the seventh day, as I was standing near a long disused house in which I had spent the night, word was brought to me that a girl, sixteen or seventeen years of age, had been killed by the tigress a few minutes previously near a village, half a mile away. From the directions given me by a party of women who had been out collecting dry sticks when the tiger had appeared, I had no difficulty in finding the place where the girl had been killed. The spot was marked by crimson splashes of blood, in vivid contrast to which were a number of bright-coloured blue beads scattered from a necklace the girl had been wearing. The blood trail from here led up, and over the top of a high hill, on the crest of which the tigress had stripped all the clothing from the girl's body.

Beyond the ridge, the hill fell steeply away, and was covered with dense scrub jungle. For a long way down this hillside, I tracked the tigress and, as I was going down a narrow and steep watercourse, I caught sight of an object some 20 yards ahead of me where the watercourse turned sharply to the right, and where there was a small pool of water. As I drew near this object, I saw it was a human leg cut off a little below the knee, as clean as though it had been severed with one blow of a sharp axe. I was puzzled to know how the tigress had accomplished this feat and, very foolishly, stooped down to examine the leg and, but for the warning conveyed to me by my Guardian Angel—or my sixth sense—my hunting of man-eaters would have ended where it began. My reaction to the warning was instantaneous and, as I grounded the butt of the rifle on the edge of the small pool and put my fingers on the triggers, the top of the 15 feet bank in front of me, dislodged by the tigress when stopping her spring, rolled down the steep bank and plopped into the pool and, as I raised my head, I heard the tigress stealing away.

The lesson I learnt that day, and learnt well, has never been forgotten, and has helped me to come safely through many adventures.

When an important and particular job is in hand, full and complete concentration on that job should never be relaxed, even for one moment, for that moment's relaxation may cost you your life, or the lives of those who are depending on you. Time and enough there will be for relaxation when the job in hand has been completed.

The full story of how the wearer of the blue beads, and those hundreds of others, was avenged has been told in a book being published by the Oxford University Press, Bombay.* The proceeds from the sale of the book are being given to that deserving institution that is trying to ameliorate the lot of those unfortunates who have been blinded in this war, and who never again will see faces, and all the beauties of nature, as you and I can see them.

* The book being referred to is *Man-Eaters of Kumaon*, first published by Oxford University Press, Bombay, in 1944. 'The spot where the girl had been killed was marked by a pool of blood and near it, in vivid contrast to the crimson pool was a broken necklace of brightly coloured blue beads which the girl had been wearing' (p. 17). *Man-Eaters of Kumaon* is still in print.

The Rudraprayag Letters

[Seventy miles north-west of Naini Tal and in the neighbouring region of Garhwal, next to Kumaon, is the town of Rudraprayag. Here the Alaknanda River is joined to the Mandakini. From 1918 to 1926 a leopard hunted here, killing both animals and human beings. By 1926, it had killed 125 people and terrorized 50,000 villagers over a 500 square mile area. A reward of Rs 10,000 was placed on the leopard's head. Repeated efforts to trap and kill it were of no avail. Despite having shot no man-eater for nearly sixteen years, Corbett offered his services which were accepted by the local administration. The hunt for the Rudraprayag man-eating leopard proved no easy task. Corbett, his team of six Garhwali porters, and his

trusted servant Madho Singh, tracked the leopard over months before meeting with success.

Below are some letters written during this time by Corbett (probably) to his sister Maggie. The letters describe in detail, typical of Corbett's writing, the long and painstaking process before the man-eating leopard of Rudraprayag was captured and killed.]

16 October 1925

Rudraprayag

Many thanks for your letter and the 'Pioneers'; its nice hearing from you every day and knowing that all is well at home. It's not often that I feel down and out, but I certainly feel that way today, and it's all my fault for having relied on another man. You remember when I fixed up with Ibbotson* to come to Rudraprayag and said when I was leaving him that I would wire to Calcutta for an electric light, and he told me that he already had one, and would have it ready for me, together with his heavy rifle and a Tahsildar to give me every assistance? Well, I wrote to him from Dwarahat telling him I was going a week ahead of him and that as I was taking my heavy rifle, I did not want his, but would be very glad to have the electric light. He received this letter alright, as also a wire I sent home from Karanprayag saying I was arriving in Rudraprayag on the 10th, and another wire from Rudraprayag saying I had arrived, and that the last kill had taken place on the 26th of September (This was just to let him know that another kill might take place at any time). On the 12th, the Patwari purchased four goats for me for fifteen rupees (the only one not pleased with the buy was old Mothi who said he used to buy Bhutia

---

* A.W. Ibbotson was deputy commissioner of Garhwal from October 1924 to March 1925. He was a great friend of Jim Corbett.

goats at four for the rupee in the olden days). I did a lot of prospecting on the 11th and 12th, and decided to take one of the two roads that meet on the west side of the river at the bridgehead. As I had no light, I did not sit up as I wanted to, and in the morning found the goat nearest the bridge killed. I tied it up where I did as I had a feeling at the back of my mind that the leopard would try and get across the bridge that night (Ibbotson's idea that the animal swims the river is all moonshine). On the 13th, I sat over the remains of the goat, and some animal came near the kill and went off without my seeing it. On the 14th, I arranged to sit up over the bridge but unfortunately changed my mind at the last moment, and sat over a live goat where the previous one had been killed. I am convinced the leopard crossed the bridge that night. On the 15th, I went for a long chakkar on the next bank and, when I was returning at about 11 a.m., was met by a man, sent by the Patwari, who informed me that a kill had taken place about 4 miles from Rudraprayag on the east bank of the river. As soon as I got to the bungalow, I sent Ibbotson an urgent wire telling him of the kill, and saying I must have the light this evening. After breakfast, I took all three of my guns and set off on the 4 mile walk. The hill goes straight up from the back of the bungalow and, in the four miles, we climbed quite 6,000 feet. The kill, or more correctly kills, for two lives were taken, was a woman. She had been caught when entering her door after washing up the pots used in the evening meal. Her cries brought her no help, and after dragging her some twenty yards by the right leg, the leopard transferred its hold to her throat and the woman's troubles were over, and another two victims added to the long list of the Rudraprayag man-eater. I found the kill in a 4 feet deep nullah running through the fields a 100 yards from the village. Thirty yards from the kill there was a big walnut tree in the branches of which there was a haystack. I looked the ground over carefully and, as it was a dark night and I had no light,

I decided to make a gun trap across the path the leopard had made the previous night when approaching and leaving the kill. I used the .275 and 28-bore loaded with some of Anderson's buck shot for the trap: but when everything was fixed up and ready, I found it required a greater pressure than the leopard was likely to exert to discharge the guns. My only hope then was to drive the leopard, and this could only be done by firing at him when he was facing the required direction. While I was engaged with the trap, two men with the help of a ladder (the tree could not be climbed owing to the platform of branches on which the rick had been made) pulled out sufficient hay from about halfway up the rick to make a place for me to sit on. By 6 p.m., everything was ready, guns nicely masked from the side the leopard was to approach, safety catches taken off, a white stone put in line with the kill to give me direction and, with the united prayers and blessings of two Patwaris, my own chaps and a hundred villagers, I climbed the rick and made myself comfortable (the ladder was of course taken away). A storm had been brewing all afternoon and, at 6.30, it burst overhead with big drops of rain the size of rupees, and some of the finest thunderclaps I have ever heard. The big drops did not give much rain and, in half an hour, the storm had gone over the ridge. The sky was however overcast and the rain had stopped.

Ten minutes later, I heard a stone drop in the nullah a little below the kill, and at the same moment it came on to rain again. I knew exactly what was going to happen—the rain had struck the leopard before it reached me, and he was coming under me for shelter. Well, for an hour or more we sat within a few feet of each other, sheltering from the rain and admiring the courage of the two men who passed some 50 yards above us on their way to the village. (I learnt afterwards that one of them was Ibbotson's man with the electric light.) At 8 of the clock, the rain gave over for good but it remained cloudy and very dark. The leopard overslept himself and did not wake up until about 3.30. He then whipped down into the lower field, dislodging some earth as he did so, crossed the nullah, and approached the kill from the side I expected him to. To make certain of his firing the trap guns, I had fixed two fishing lines, instead of the usual one thread used on these occasions, and he evidently got his head between them and took fright, for he sprang off the hill, dashed along a field for 60 or 70 yards and then growled. I knew he would get over his fright in time so just sat tight and, half an hour later, the white stone had disappeared. I had not counted on this happening; the stone had been placed to give me something to aim at when I heard him eating, and to drive him if I missed into the trap. With the stone obscured, there was no earthly chance of hitting him and still less chance, as I did not know in which direction his head was, of sending him into the fish lines. While I was trying to think what I should do, the stone suddenly appeared in sight and I heard and saw the leopard come straight towards me and disappear under the hay rick. He had passed within 3 feet of the trap guns, which were quite exposed on the side, without taking the least notice of them. You will have noticed that I *heard* the leopard. It was the strangest sound for an animal to make that I have ever heard, just like a woman walking in a very stiff silk dress. How the sound was made I can't imagine; it was loud enough to be heard distinctly at 30 yards. From the fact of my being able to see him, I conclude he is a very old animal with a skin about the colour of straw. He is not a very long leopard but stands high and is very heavily built. I now thought I had a very good chance of bagging him; he was certain to go back the way he came and would give me a more or less easy shot. The minutes dragged by until thirty must have passed, my heart was beating in my throat and

I was dying to cough and then, without my having seen anything, the white stone again disappeared and shortly after the leopard came a second time straight towards me. Another interval of half an hour and, as the stone disappeared, I made up my mind, through stress of circumstances, for a time was coming when I simply must cough or choke, that when he next came towards me I must chance a shot. On this occasion, he ate for some considerable time but I had not coughed and was ready for him, and as he passed right under me, I leant forward and fired. The field he was in was perhaps two, or possibly two and a half feet wide, and I planted a .450 bullet right in the middle of it and all that happened, or rather all the injury I did the leopard was to cut a few hairs from his neck. The village turned out as was only to be expected, and I spent the remainder of the night in the Pradhan's hut. And so the story of my failure ends, failure that is entirely due to my having been assured that I would find an electric torch waiting for me at Rudraprayag. I may get a second chance at the expense of another human life, but the conditions will not be so favourable. With the most vivid lightning there was that night, I might have shone an electric light on the leopard for minutes at a time without it paying any attention, and you know, and I know, that in the brilliant light that torchlight gives, I could never have missed a huge thing like a leopard at ten feet. I am writing to Ibbotson and am telling him that the killing of the most valuable horse in Garhwal would have been a cheap price to pay for the destruction of the man-eater. The man who brought the light covered 28 miles in 7 hours, a truly wonderful feat. A horse would have done the distance in 5 hours at the most, and the 2 hours saved would have rid Garhwal of a devil that has terrified the country for seven years.

Have no fears about me, I am taking no chances and allow the men with me to take none.

20 October 1925
Rudraprayag

Nothing has happened since I last wrote to you. I had a goat killed on the 18th, its head had been crushed and there were no other marks on it. I sat up the following night and nothing happened. The people here say the man-eater often kills goats but does not eat them. I am getting letters from people in Garhwal thanking me for having come, and wherever I go, people come out and bless me for being here. It is most embarrassing, especially as I will have to wait until one of them is killed before I can do anything. The Lord knows if I will be able to hit the beast when I see him again. His habits are unlike other leopards, he never comes out until the *chirags*† are lit, and is away long before it gets light in the morning. So, without a kill one can't do anything. No one is afraid in daylight. In the miles and miles I have walked, I have found women and quite small children cutting grass or collecting wood in all sorts of out-of-the-way and fearfully dangerous places, and they have not shown the least bit of fear even when I have come upon them suddenly. But all that is changed when dusk comes on them, and everyone is afraid of the terror that walks by night. By the way, I wonder whether there were man-eaters in the olden days!

As I have said before, don't have any fears for me. I take no risks night or day and can't do more than I am doing for my own safety and the safety of the men with me.

23 October 1925
Rudraprayag

... Nothing has happened since I wrote to you on the 21st. One feels so helpless with this beast that kills but won't eat ordinary animals.

† Earthenware lamps with oil and a wick.

All I can do is to wait for another human kill and, as soon as one takes place, I will pack up my things and whether I get a shot or not that night, I will start for home next morning. If the people did not have such implicit faith in me, and if it did not mean so much to Garwhal, I would have started on the return journey the morning after I missed the leopard.

26 October 1925
Rudraprayag

Many thanks for your letter of the 22nd received this morning. I was beginning to feel anxious about you all, and called in at the Post Office on my way back from a *chakkar* (round) with the intention of wiring if there was no post from you. Then I met nice old Mothi near the office with your letter.

I am afraid the leopard has left these parts. I traced him for some distance this morning along the path he took the night after I fired at him, and am relieved to think he is somewhere between Sivannand and Chattapepal on the Karanprayag road. I have sent two goats to be tied up near Sivannand tonight and, after I have seen Ibbotson on the 28th, will go up in that direction myself. There is a bridge at Sivannand and a bridge at Chattapepal, both of which I have had closed from the 16th with the idea of confining the leopard to this bank, and it is possible he has gone upriver with the intention of crossing one of these bridges. The bridge here I close every evening with thorn bushes.

★ ★ ★

Two rivers meet here, the Alaknanda from Badrinath and the Mandargavri from Kedarnath (I don't think the river is called the Ganges until it passes Hardwar). I have tried both rivers and have not caught a single fish. The people here tell me the fish come up in thousands in April and go down in September. There is a lovely pool just under the bungalow, and the Mission School master, who has been here two years, says it simply swarms with fish, some of them as big as a man, in April and May. Someday I must come and see if these reports are true.

31 October 1925

Rudraprayag

The cake has arrived safely, many thanks for it. I had dinner with the Ibbotsons on the 28th, and they left for Agastmani the following morning. He has gone up to settle some land dispute and will probably return on the 2nd, do a bird shoot with me on the 3rd, and leave for Pauri on the 4th. He sent me his file regarding the electric light some days ago. From it I see he issued orders as soon as he got back from Naini for the light to be sent to me. There was a little delay in finding it, and eventually at 12 o'clock on the 14th, a chaprasi was dispatched from Pauri with instructions to deliver the light to me without any loss of time. On receipt of my wire of the 15th, he was assured that the light had gone the previous day and must have reached me. In his statement, the chaprasi says he arrived at Rudraprayag at 11 o'clock on the 15th, lost his way to Gwar village where the kill was, arrived at the village at 6.30 when it was quite dark, and handed the light over to my men who refused to take it to me where I was sitting up! I left for Gwar at 1 p.m. on the 15th, and if the chaprasi had arrived at 11 o'clock, he would have found me here. As a matter of fact, he never came to Rudraprayag at all. The *halkara* who left here with the post at 1.10 p.m. states he met the chaprasi and a Gwar villager at Panch-bhai-khal, 3 miles from here. The villager was on his way back from Sirinagar, and the *halkara* had great pleasure in telling him all about the kill. Panch-bhai-Khal is two and a half miles from Gwar along quite a good road, and what the beast of a chaprasi did from say 2.10 to 7.30 p.m. (the time he actually arrived) I can't for the life of me think. One would imagine that, as they were going to a village where there was a man-eater, they would have tried to get there as early in the day as possible. What they probably did was to wait at Gali, an intermediate village in the hope of going up with someone who was going in their direction. If I had known as much that night as I know now, I would have tied the chaprasi near the kill and chanced it. Of one thing I am glad, and that is that a Garhwali and not a white man will be responsible for all the kills that take place from now on.

Ibbotson is a good chap and is even more disappointed than I am, if that is possible, at my not having got the leopard that night. He did all he could about the light, and it was not his fault that it reached me two hours late.

3 November 1925
Rudraprayag

The Ibbotsons are back from Agastmani and have asked me to dine with them tonight. They don't mind my going to dinner in shorts, and Ibbotson wears them himself; so everyone is comfortable and happy. They will probably stay here until the 6th morning and I am trying to arrange two days' bird shooting. I have seen lots of pheasants but the going is bad and it is very difficult to get men; however, I have my own ten men, and if I can get another five, we should make something of a bag. I have shot a kaker and a ghooral since I last wrote to you, both at long ranges. The rifle appears to be shooting better since Peacock fixed the silver sight to it. The bone sight came off last winter if you remember, and lost me that leopard the evening we were coming down the Dalhousie villas road. Silver shows up better than bone, and should be used for all sporting rifles. Manton said they were sending a silver sight but I have not opened their parcel yet—but there is no reason why I should not open it now—that is the best of a tent, everything is so handy. Yes—it is a silver sight and better if anything than the one I have on the rifle. However, I will stick to the old one until I get back home.

4 November 1925
Rudraprayag

News has just come of a cow kill 5 miles from here. Ibbotson won't hear of taking a shot, but is coming to make tea for me and hear the fun. The leopard might, by a great stroke of luck, be the man-eater, but I have my doubts.

23 March 1926
Rudraprayag

The leopard is on this bank of the river, and on the 20th a cow was killed half a mile from the bungalow. The leopard was unable to get the kill through the door (it killed the cow inside a hut in which there were three other cows) and only ate its neck and head. We sat up on the 21st in our patent haystack, which was made proof against attack by yards upon yards of wire netting. The leopard came alright at about 7.30, but evidently heard us and went off. At midnight, we were escorted back to the bungalow by a gang of men with lights and, after we had left, the leopard returned and had a small meal. Yesterday, we made a small window in a wall overlooking the kill and sat up inside the house all night. The moon set at about 2 a.m. and, two hours later, I heard the leopard eating. The next second, a man coughed in an adjoining room. For 10 minutes there was no sound and, just as I again heard it, it came on to rain. At 4.30, the rain was over and, as I was watching the kill through a small hole in the curtain we had hung in front of the window, I thought I could see something near the kill. The light improved every second, and it was not long before I could distinctly see the leopard sitting up facing our way. I was moving my rifle a couple of inches to take a shot when a woman passed our house with a torch in her hand to milk the cows in a hut just below us. The leopard of course disappeared like a flash and, as it was then daylight, we came back to a warm bath and *chhota hazri*.

27 March 1926

Rudraprayag

I am so sorry to learn from your letter of the 23rd received today that you have not had any of my letters—this is the fourth I have written you since we arrived here.

We sat up in our cabin over the bridge last night, and came back at 10.30 p.m. to a bath and a hot cup of cocoa. At 7 a.m. this morning, a man came in to report that a woman and her baby six months old had been mauled in a village about 3 miles away. The door of the house in which the woman and her family were sleeping opened inwards and closed on her as the leopard was trying to pull her out. The woman's arm was badly bitten and her breast and back torn, and the kid got a claw into its head. We gave what medicine we could, but it is unlikely the woman will escape blood poisoning. After breakfast, I went out to see if I could catch a fish. The Nandagani that joins the Ganges just below the bungalow is about the size of the Kosi at Khairna. Half a mile up, I saw a small *mahaseer* so put the rod together and had a try with a medium spoon, and in an hour and a half I landed three fish, 15 pounds, 5 pounds, and 36 pounds. I came straight back after killing the 36-pounder and, when we had had lunch, Ibbotson and I went back to the pool and within a few minutes killed another beauty weighing 25 pounds. Not bad for one day's fishing in strange waters, was it? Tomorrow being Sunday, we propose to have a whole day's fishing. Am running short of cigarettes, can you please send me two tins?

P.S. 7 a.m., 28 March 1926: Word has just come in that a cow was killed last night in a village two miles from where the woman was mauled, so there will be no fishing for us today.

4 April 1926
Rudraprayag

No letter from you for two days, I hope all at home are well.

We have had bad luck these last few days or rather, the leopard has had its usual good luck. On Thursday morning, we heard it had called all night just above the bazaar and, while we were having breakfast, a man came to say it was lying on a rock sunning itself just above a village, a quarter of a mile from here. We went off on foot, and searched for two hours without result. In the afternoon, we took a goat and sat up until sundown. The goat was a silent one, like all its kind here, so I called twice. The goat was above us on the hill and, at my second call, it jumped up and took a great interest in something further up the hill where we could not see. Nothing further happened, so we untied the goat and started for the village. The goat kept getting between our legs, so we let it loose and it dashed off up the hill. As it would not allow itself to be caught, we left it behind and found, two days later, that it had been killed just where we gave up trying to catch it. Just killed and left. On Friday morning, word came in that a man had been killed the previous night at 8 o'clock in a village 400 yards from where we had sat over the goat. We poisoned the body with Cameron's poison[‡] and did not sit up (There were no convenient trees near the kill; in fact, there were no trees at all anywhere near the kill). Next morning (Saturday), we found the kill had been carried off 200 yards and a lot eaten, with the poisoned parts carefully avoided. We put more poison in, and

‡ Cyanide

that night I sat up on a tree near a path he had used the previous nights. At about 8 o'clock, I heard some animal, but it did not sound like a leopard. There was no moon, and it was pitch dark owing to heavy clouds. A little later, a kaker called in the direction of the kill (By the way, I have forgotten to say I was about 250 yards from the kill). The moon came up about midnight, and though it remained cloudy, it was quite light enough for me to see to shoot anything that came along the path. At 1 o'clock, I was dying to cough, and as I had to make some noise, I called like a leopard.§ At 2 o'clock, the leopard came down the hill onto the path, and when within 2 yards of where I could have seen him, he quickly left the path and walked right under my tree and, after having a drink in the stream, went up the opposite hill. I am convinced he did not know I was within miles of him, and it was special providence or good luck that made him leave the path and pass me in the one place it was impossible for me to see him. Ibbotson was sitting up in a tree some distance down the hill and did not see or hear anything. There was still a hope that he had eaten the poison, a hope that was strengthened by the fact that he had gone away at 2 a.m. instead of at 7 as he had done the previous morning (The villagers had seen him crossing the hill). Ibbotson met me as soon as it was daylight, and we went to have a look at the kill. It had been dragged some

§ Corbett is well-known for having mastered the art of mimicking a tiger's growls. He often used it to 'call up' a tiger by imitating another one so as 'to fool the intended beast into thinking that the false sound is not a man but a possible mate or a territorial intruder ... Over a kill, or in the mating season, he would growl possessively or call enticingly, as the occasion demanded. He seldom failed to bring himself the tiger or tigress he already knew to be in the area' (Martin Booth, 1986, *Carpet Sahib: A Life of Jim Corbett*, Oxford University Press, pp. 192–3).

distance, and one dose of the poison eaten. We came home to have a bit of breakfast and, at midday, set off with 300 men to beat the leopard out. I took up a position across a valley where I could command the opposite hill and get shots at from 200 to 300 yards, and Ibbotson went with the beat. At 2 p.m., the beaters appeared on the ridge in front, and Ibbotson shouted across that two men had joined him who reported that a man had been killed the previous night at a village 7 miles on the far side of the river. He also said he had found some caves, with the fresh marks of the man-eater at the mouth of one of them. After I joined him, we sent four of our own men to verify the report of the fresh kill, and went back with twenty men to seal up the cave. It had been raining all day and going on the steep hill was bad. By 5 p.m., we had closed the caves and when we returned to the bungalow, we sent off four more men to bring *khabar* of the reported kill. This morning, six men who left the village where the kill is said to have taken place at midnight arrived while we were having chhota hazri and stated that the body had not been found, so we are now waiting to hear what news our men bring back. It is not possible that the man-eater who walked under me at 2 a.m. would have gone off to a village 7 miles away and killed a man before daylight, and yet there is the disappearance of the man to account for. The door of the cattle shed he was sleeping in was found open, and his blanket outside with marks of a drag for some distance. One thing is certain, and that is the poison is non-effective as is proved from the digested toes at the mouth of the cave. We are going to keep the caves closed for forty-eight hours, and then put wire netting a little distance from the openings, remove the stones, and sit over them in turn, and if anything appears, close them up for the night and repeat the programme until something does happen, or there is another kill on this side. The leopard has never taken to the river up to this point, and the bridge here, and at Chattapepal

10 miles upstream, have been carefully closed every night since the 16th. As you will see from the above, this animal appears to have more than a 30 kazza¶ to account for his being alive this present day of 4th April 1926.

10 a.m. The post is in, and I am very glad to have your letter of the 31st and to know all is well at home. If the McWatters are not satisfied with Grasmere, they can take another house and greatly oblige us. I am glad you have asked sanction for the saplings at Hatton Hall. I promised Stiffe the court would be ready by April. The next time you see Gill, you might ask him if he has any more old lamp posts— the kind we used for the Hill Crest tennis court— which could be put between the saplings.

I hope you got my letter asking for cigarettes. I am beginning to feel hungry for a smoke—my own fault for not having written until I had run out of the supply I bought.

7 April 1926

Rudraprayag

Our monsoon is still going strong. It usually clears up in the morning, gets overcast by midday, and rains in sheets at night…. There is no further news of the missing man. Six hundred men searching for three days have failed to find any trace of him. Dirty dishes to show he had eaten his evening meal, a blanket caught in the closing door and a few stones dislodged by some heavy object having been dragged over them, and there the matter ends, possibly for all time. That he was killed by some animal appears to be beyond a shadow of doubt, but I am not inclined to think the man-eater we are hunting on this side of the river had anything to do with the killing. Nor am I inclined to think there are two man-eaters. That the man-eater

¶ Its time had not come.

was at our kill from 8 p.m. to 2 a.m., I am quite certain. How then to account for the disappearance of a man 7 miles away on the same night is beyond me.

I spent yesterday in putting wire netting in front of the caves we have closed up, and after lunch today we will have the stones removed and sit over them for three or four hours, and if nothing comes out we will close them before coming away and try again tomorrow.

11 April 1926

Rudraprayag

Many thanks for the cake and cigarettes, we made our dinner off the former last night. Ibbotson had made arrangements to go to Powri yesterday to replenish stores and see to some urgent work, and just as he was starting, word came that a woman had been killed at a village about 2 miles away. We went to the spot after breakfast and found that an old woman of eighty-five had been killed at daylight at the door of a house right in the middle of quite a large village. The body had been dragged about a quarter of a mile and carefully hidden under a medlar tree. As there were no trees for a sit-up, we decided to set a gun trap and supplement it with a big gun trap, and while Ibbotson returned to Rudraprayag for the extra guns, grub, and so on, I did a cast round. I am convinced I hit on the place the leopard was lying at, but although there was only light scrub jungle with cultivated land on two sides and the river and open clear forest on the other two, I failed to get a shot at the beast. Ibbotson returned at 2 p.m., and by 4.30 we had all our arrangements made. A string connecting the body with the triggers of the two rifles and the trap set 20 feet away and a little below the kill. The body had been dragged from south to north, and it was reasonable to suppose that if it was dragged any further, it would be taken in the same direction, but to make quite sure we planted some strong thorn bushes on the south side. At 5 p.m. we had finished our tea-dinner off the cake and a tin of fruit and climbed into our *machan*. The machan was about 7 feet square, and made high up in a beautiful old mango tree on the village side of the ravine, about 60 yards in a direct line from the kill. We made ourselves comfortable and as long as it was light, I watched the opposite hill in the hope the leopard would show up and give me a shot. Nothing, however, showed up and, as the light died out in the west, it came on to rain. The rain gave out after a bit, and I looked at my watch and found it was 7.15. Five minutes later, there was a succession of angry growls from the direction of the kill—the leopard had walked into the trap. In less time than it takes to tell, we had roused the village and fifty men came along with pine torches and we started off to stalk the trap—it was empty when we got to it, a bunch of hair and teeth marks on the iron was all there was to show the leopard had been in it. The trap weighs over a *maund*, and it had been dragged right out of the hole we had buried it in, so the leopard had evidently had some difficulty in freeing itself, but he had got out safely and the hair he lost was from the side of his foot. The kill had been dragged towards the rifles and, in order to do this, the bushes we had planted had been torn up out of the ground. Every scrap of the poor old woman had been eaten. By 8 p.m., we were back in the machan, or cabin as Ibbotson called it (It was fixed all round with wire netting and a kettle, teapot, lamps, and a hundred other things were hung all round). The kettle was soon boiling on the blue flame stove and, after a few smokes, we settled down for the night. The kill was a quarter of a mile to the north of the village; our way home lay to the south. At daylight, we took down the two rifles we had fixed in the tree, gave the relations permission to dispose of the body, and started off home. A hundred yards from our tree, there was a scratch mark and, from there right back to Rudraprayag and within a few yards of the bungalow, there were fourteen scratch

25 July 1875-19 April 1955

Jim Corbett with the Bachelor of Powalgarh

Corbett's 'Irish cottage', Kaladhungi, Uttar Pradesh, India

'Although Jim Corbett was a naturalist and a shikari par excellence … he was one of the first initiates of wild life conservation in India.' —The Sunday Statesman

'On a good day I have seen eighteen varieties brought to the bag ranging from snipe …'

'[Corbett] delight[s], with descriptions in minute and often credible detail of the way of birds, reptiles and animals, and how to observe and interpret the sights, sounds and smells of the jungle. . . . We may be thankful to [Corbett] for sharing a little of it with us, and for allowing us to accompany him on his expeditions.'
—The Indian Express

Jim Corbett (second from right) with his family, Naini Tal, c. 1900

At Nyeri, Kenya, 1955

Corbett's grave at the St Peter's Anglican Church cemetery, Nyeri, Kenya

Jim Corbett at Paxtu in Kenya with a White Eye on his hand

JIM CORBETT

In token of the affection and esteem of all who knew you
and of the many whom you set on the right path in

14 INDIAN DIVISION
1944-45

Bengali edition of
The Temple Tiger

At Nyeri, Kenya, 1954

marks. The road is mostly red mud; the rain had softened it, and the pugs of the leopard were as distinct as photographs, all four feet were quite sound so the trap had done him no harm. While Ibbotson was having a bite, I followed the tracks down the Powri road. A quarter of a mile from the bungalow, some Bhootias were camped in the middle of the road; the leopard had walked right into the camp and killed one of their goats.

20 April 1926
Rudraprayag
I am sorry to learn from your letters that the monsoon has extended to Naini. However, as the storms are all from the north-west, I hope they have expended most of their force before they reach you. The wind we have had here during the past twenty-four hours would have blown the roof off any house in Naini.

Ibbotson has been in Powri since the 14th, and will probably return today or tomorrow. I have had three visitors lately—no, four. The Monros 14th to 16th; Duke and Army chap from Rourkee, 16th; Cobb, also from Rourkee, 17th; and the Civil Surgeon Powri 18th and 19th (I don't know this chap's name). Duke and Cobb were anxious to break journey here, but their men refused to stay so they had to push on to the next stage 10 miles away. Both are on their way to the river to try to get some *tahr*** shooting. Duke is trying to keep ahead of Cobb to get the cream of the shooting.

24 April 1926
Rudraprayag
Many thanks for the money and cake. Ibbotson enjoys the cakes as much as I do and we have nothing else for our afternoon teas. I have

** A large wild goat

been out of touch with the leopard for several days. On the 20th, I sat up for a few hours half a mile from the bungalow. The leopard came onto the road a hundred yards from where I was sitting, sometime between 7–8 p.m., and scratched ten times between my tree and the bungalow, and went on right through the bazaar. Since then, I have not been able to find any trace of him. It will be a full moon soon, and I don't think there will be any killing for at least another week.

29 April 1926
Rudraprayag

… I have had no luck since last writing to you. After killing the goat I told you about and two more the following night, the leopard went straight off to a village 18 miles away and killed a boy of fifteen. I sat up the whole night, but from the first had no hope of seeing the leopard as the villagers had driven it off the previous night and recovered the body. The night before last I sat over a goat, and at 7.30 p.m., heard two leopards fighting. I called them up, and the next time they fought, they were only 30 yards from my tree. I was afraid to call again for fear they should see me, and as the beastly goat did not call, they went on up the hill and I did not hear them again. Judging from the noises, the male was a very big animal and may have been the man-eater. The moon is well up, and there are not likely to be any human kills for the next week or ten days.

Corbett on *The Man-Eating Leopard of Rudraprayag*

[*The Man-Eating Leopard of Rudraprayag* was published in 1948, twenty years after the chase described in the letters given above. While many have been impressed with Corbett's powers of recall, there is no evidence to suggest that at the time of writing *The Man-Eating Leopard of Rudraprayag*, Corbett had access to the letters written two decades earlier. The following letters to his publisher reveal Corbett having taken pains to 'tell it as he actually saw it'.—Editor]

… I finished the Rudraprayag story last evening and took the last chapter to a friend's house, to try it out. I had an audience of three, a man, his wife, and their daughter of twenty. After I had finished reading, the man blew his nose and said in a husky voice: 'splendid', and the girl said, 'Mother and I are crying too much to be able to say anything'. I did not write the book with the intention of making people cry, but perhaps it will not affect others in the same way. I am not clever enough to paint a word picture with any but the words at my command, not have I the art of creating imaginary scenes. So when I tell a story I try and tell it as I actually saw it, and if I were to leave out all the tragic scenes, the resulting story would be flat and meaningless.

—Jim Corbett, 27 August 1946; quoted in Roy E. Hawkin's letter to
Geoffrey J. Cumberlege, Publisher, Oxford University Press,
5 November 1946

… I have sent your copy of *The Man-Eating Leopard of Rudraprayag* to Hawkins for despatch to you. Sit by your fire some evening when it is snowing and read the book, and let me have your reactions to it. Hawkins thinks that some of my statements on jungle lore will result in a lot of controversy. I am quite prepared for this, and know that my statements are right, and that no one can prove me wrong. If Hawkins sends you half of the photographs I have sent him, you will have lots to choose from.

—Jim Corbett's letter to L.B., 28 January 1947

My dear Cumberlege,
Your letter of 10th April arrived while the doctors and nurses of our local hospital were struggling to pull me back from heaven, which I all but reached in spite of their combined efforts, so please forgive the delay in answering it.

Hawkins and Mrs Carrick have given me their opinion of the new book, and I now have your opinion, and as all three of you think it is better than the old book I have no anxiety about it; for though you are my friends, I know you have given me what I wanted, your honest opinions.

I agree with you that the title I have chosen is over-long, and that people outside India will find it difficult to pronounce the word 'Rudraprayag'. To avoid this difficulty, I thought of calling the book 'The Man-eater of Garhwal', but finally decided that this would not be an appropriate title for a book dealing with an animal that had for many years been known throughout India as the Rudraprayag man-eater. The insertion of a hyphen would possibly solve the difficulty of pronunciation, Rudra-prayag.

I know my interests are in very good hands and I am very grateful for all you have done for me.

—Jim Corbett's letter to Geoffrey J. Cumberlege, written
from Gurney House, Naini Tal, 20 June 1947

The Making of Corbett's *My India*: Correspondence with his Editors
[From the OUP archives]

My dear Hawkins,

Many thanks for your letters ... of 5th and 9th July. I was glad to see from these two letters that you were back in Bombay for, not having seen your signature for so long, I was afraid you had gone off to one of the distant OUP branches, where I would have lost touch with you. The Bombay you have returned to will be very different from the Bombay you left a year ago. However, I hope that you and your staff, whom I had the pleasure of meeting while on my way through Bombay, will find life under the changed conditions not too unbearable.

... It is very gratifying to know that the book [*The Man-Eaters of Kumaon*] is having such a long run ... and I am receiving letters of thanks from people who have read *Rudraprayag*. Answering these letters is hanging up *My India*, but I have written a few chapters which I will send you, and on which I would like you to give me your opinion. The book will be in two parts: the first part dealing with village life in Kumaon, and the second part with my work in Bengal. If I can write the book as I shall like to, I am hoping it will be read by those to whom *Man-Eaters* did not appeal. No, that last sentence is not correct, for I am writing the book in response to readers of *Man-Eaters* who have asked for more information about the poor of India. What I do mean is that I hope the people who were not interested in sport will be interested in the people of India. Not all the requests for a book on this subject have come from America; many have come from the UK, Canada, Australia, and from other parts of the world.

I don't know if you ever met John Slavery, who for many years was sub-editor of *The Pioneer*, and who was also connected with other papers in India and at home. After reading both my books, he said the second was far better than the first, and later, when I showed him some of the American reviews, he said they were just what he expected, and that they were the best reviews on any books he had ever seen. In his opinion, one review alone, by a world renowned woman reviewer, would sell 100,000 copies of the book. I hope he will prove to be right, and I hope you will not think I have done wrong to thank this person for her splendid review.

—Jim Corbett's letter to Roy E. Hawkins from

Nyeri, Kenya, 23 July 1948

My dear Corbett,

I was particularly glad to see you are [back] on your typewriter by the letter of 23 July which arrived this morning, for only yesterday I was asked to confirm or deny the rumour that you were back in

India! For the present, I am sure you are much better off where you are!

It is very good news to hear [that] you are working on *My India*, and I am sure there are thousands of people who will be glad to have it. Comparatively few women, specially, feel the excitement of the chase—at least in a book—and they have been readers of *Man-Eaters* and *The Leopard* under protest, as it were, to be able to know what their husbands are so excited about. But the background of Indian village life in your books delights nearly all readers. I should guess that the new book may well have a wider appeal than either of its predecessors ...

—Roy E. Hawkins' letter to Jim Corbett,

3 August 1948

My dear Corbett,

... I am very glad to hear [*My India*] is making such good progress. No, I have never heard of the infamous Sultana,* and am therefore looking forward all the more to reading your story of him. Provided you state that your account is based on memory, no one can complain if some of the details vary from those recorded in the police files, and I am quite sure you are right not to ask for a copy of Freddy Young's report if that is likely to spoil your story. The middle way

---

* 'Sultana: India's Robin Hood' forms Chapter 9 of Jim Corbett's *My India*. It tells the story of the capture of the dacoit Sultana, a member of the Bhantu criminal tribe, who rarely robbed the poor and eluded government agencies for three long years. At the request of Freddy Young, a police officer in the United Provinces, Corbett joined many hunts organized to trace him. He was finally caught and, 'with his brave demeanour, won the respect of those who guarded him in his condemned cell' (Jim Corbett, 1952, *My India*, Oxford University Press, p. 130).

would be for you to read the report only after you have written your account, so that you would be able to make any changes which made for accuracy provided they did not spoil the story....

—Roy E. Hawkins' letter to Jim Corbett,
31 August 1948

My dear Hawkins,

Herewith, the first five chapters of *My India*.

I should like you to take the manuscript home with you and read it in the quiet of your own house, which I visited when Chester was living in it, and then let me know what you think of it.

I have made an exact copy of the manuscript, and if you have any suggestions to make, or would like any particular word to be altered, you need only quote the page and line number. I am hoping, however, that you will not suggest any major alterations for I have recounted, as best as I could, true incidents without any embellishments.

I felt terribly annoyed at my request for government recognition of Harwa and Narwa being turned down, for I felt at the time, and still feel, that if they had not belonged to the depressed class, their case would have received sympathetic treatment. However, if you feel that the last para on Page 68 [of the manuscript of *My India*] should be toned down, or omitted, I will raise no objection. I could of course have appealed to the Governor or the Viceroy, but in doing so I would have been appealing against their own rules, and if either of them had admitted my appeal, it might have resulted in making a very embarrassing precedent.

The following para from a letter just received from Jarvis, one-time Governor of Sinai and a regular contributor of *Country Life*, will interest you.

I can't remember if I wrote to you about the 'Man-eating Leopard' which arrived by airmail shortly after your letter. I have read it andso have all the family and others who liked [Man-Eaters of] Kumaon so much, and the general opinion, with which I concur, is that it is right up to the standard of that book—which is a very high standard. I won't say it is better since I am doubtful if you could get anything better than *Kumaon*. The extraordinary thing about your big-game books is that women enjoy reading them as much as men, and the average woman would not dream of reading an ordinary big-game book ...

—Jim Corbett's letter to Roy E. Hawkins from
Nyeri, Kenya, 1 September 1948

My dear Corbett,

I read your first four chapters soon after they arrived, and again last night, and am sure that you are writing another book which is going to be very widely appreciated. Until your MS is complete, I don't think any suggestions are likely to be useful. Up to the present, the only thing I feel strongly is that your first chapter is too long—I was impatient to hear your stories, and did not want to linger on the top of Cheena. All good storytellers keep you waiting during which time your impatience and eagerness to know what is going to happen next pile up, but it is a bit dangerous to start a book with such a waiting period. However, all I want to say is that I like Chapters II–IV very much indeed, and shall eagerly look forward to reading the rest.

—Roy E. Hawkins' letter to Jim Corbett,
27 September 1948

My dear Hawkins,

I am very glad you like the first few chapters of our third book [*My India*]. As soon as my sister leaves hospital and settles down in our cottage, and can do things for herself, I will take the remaining five chapters in hand.

I am hoping that *Rudraprayag* and *My India* will appeal to Indians even more than *Man-Eaters* did. If this should prove to be so, I

sincerely hope you will consider bringing out a cheap Urdu edition
that will be within the reach of 'the poor of India' ...

—Jim Corbett's letter to Roy E. Hawkins from Nyeri, Kenya,

27 September 1948

My dear Hawkins,

... *My India* is ready, and I am sending it to you by airmail. I should
like you to read the typescript; put it aside for a week, read it again,
and then let me know what you think of it. Most of the requests
I have received for more information about India and her people
have come from America, and further. America and India are
our best customers. I should like you to bear this in mind when
reading the typescript. I hope you will not think the book too
short; but if you do, I could add a final chapter of from five to ten
thousand words. In this chapter, I would describe life in general in
Mokameh Ghat—the school Ram Saran and I started—Christmas
morning when I distributed 80 per cent of the profit I made during
the year among the staff and my men—inter-railway hockey
and football matches—one or two interesting snake stories, and
so on...

—Jim Corbett's letter to Roy E. Hawkins from Nyeri, Kenya,

22 October 1949

My dear Corbett,

Our letters crossed—you have anticipated what was wanted and I
shall look forward to seeing the last chapter of *My India*.... I am
very glad to see your writing again, all the more so because one
S.N. Aggarwal sent us a postcard from Bihar last week which started
with the words: 'I have just heard a rumour that Col Jim Corbett
has been killed by some wild animal'. I reassured him by saying that

certainly the newspapers would have reported any such incident, but I feel pretty sure that telepathic communication does take place occasionally, so it is pleasant to be sure.

Yes, I think you are responsible for the revival of the *Man-eaters of Tsavo*† and for the other books which are appearing. Let us hope your example will encourage people to tackle the man-eaters which, as you say, are now pretty frequently reported in India. The Provincial Government does not seem to be able to make up its mind on the subject: on the one hand they are encouraging cultivators to shoot at anything anytime, in order to protect their crops and 'grow more food'; but on the other, they have declared one or two areas to be National Parks, in which all wildlife is to be preserved. But with so many inexperienced people trying to shoot tigers and panthers, evidently plenty of wounded animals are escaping to become man-eaters....

—Letter by Roy E. Hawkins to Jim Corbett in Nyeri, Kenya,
6 April 1950

My dear Cumberlege,

... I am glad to know there is a prospect of *My India* being published in the near future. Not a day passes without my receiving enquiries about this book, and people in all parts of the world tell me they

---

† *The Man-eaters of Tsavo and other East African Adventures* by J.H. Patterson was published in 1907. The book recounts the author's experiences while overseeing the construction of a railroad bridge in Kenya. It is most widely known for recounting the story of a pair of lions, known as the Tsavo man-eaters, which he killed. After Jim Corbett's *Man-Eaters of Kumaon* was published by Oxford University Press in 1944, the earlier title gained a new lease of life.

have registered their names for a copy. I most sincerely hope that our friends will not be disappointed with the book, and I also hope reviewers will be as kind to us as they have hitherto been. One adverse review, like some I have seen on other books, would kill me outright. I have no uneasiness about the Indian reception, but I am not so sure about the UK and the USA. However, in writing books, as in other things, it is unwise to look for trouble....

—Jim Corbett's letter from Nyeri, Kenya to
Geoffrey Cumberlege, 25 January 1951

My dear Corbett,

Thank you for your letter.... I did not realize you were so keen on early publication of *My India*, but will see if it can be speeded up. But publication seems to take longer and longer, and know that our New York Office has made most of its plans for 1951 already. I expect it has kept a place for *My India*, but it does not seem possible to launch a book successfully without lengthy preparation....

—Letter to Jim Corbett in Nyeri, Kenya by Roy E. Hawkins,
24 August 1950

My dear Hawkins,

...I am very sorry to learn from your letter...that there is no possibility of *My India* being published this year. I know many other people will be as disappointed, as I shall be, at not being able to give the book as a 1950 Christmas present. Putting back the publication of this book will mean putting back the publication of *Jungle Lore*, which I shall greatly regret, for I wanted to see this last book of mine in print...

—Jim Corbett's letter from Nyeri, Kenya to Roy E. Hawkins,
18 August 1950

My dear Hawkins,

Many thanks for your letter.... With the difference that you are an expert and I am an amateur, our interests in *My India* are the same, and while I should like the book to be published in 1950, I will not question your decision to publish it in 1951, so please do not upset the arrangements you have made....

—Jim Corbett's letter from Nyeri, Kenya to Roy. E. Hawkins,

24 August 1950

My dear Hawkins,

... I am anxiously looking forward to your presentation of *My India*. The nearer we approach the date of publication, the more nervous I get. I am very conscious of my shortcomings and sincerely hope that the critics will deal gently with me. So far we have had no adverse reviews on our books, and if they start now, I will feel that I have let everybody down. The letters I have had from people ... are very encouraging, and all the letters are not from friends. The rumour that I have been killed by lions has started again and some of the letters of enquiry, to banks and others, give me a dry feeling in my throat ...

—Jim Corbett's letter from Nyeri, Kenya to Roy E. Hawkins,

28 March 1952

My dear Hawkins,

I have not seen your signature for a long time and I am wondering if at this moment you are sitting in an office chair in Bombay, or indulging in winter sports in Switzerland. Leave rules for you do not appear to be as generous as they are for people in this country.

Book catalogues just received in Kenya announce that *My India* is to be published in March. When your copies are ready, I would like you to send, to debit of my account, a copy to each of the following:

Pundit Nehru

Pundit Govind Ballabh Pant, Prime Minister, U.P.

Maharaj Singh, Governor, Bombay

Babu Jagat Singh Negi, Gurney House, Naini Tal, U.P.

Shri V. R. Pathak, Birla Vidiamandir, Naini Tal, U.P. ...

—Letter from Jim Corbett in Nyeri, Kenya to
Roy E. Hawkins, 22 January 1952

My India: Reviews

This is a book which must hold its readers spellbound. The author has a complete hold on the story, the incidents read well and are as interesting as a book of fiction written by a first-rate author, he is intensely humane, natural, and sympathetic...

—File Note, Oxford University Press, Bombay Branch,
18 August 1951

Sir,

I wonder how many of those who are familiar with Jim Corbett have read his book *My India*. I say so because, unlike the author's other books, it is not primarily a book about adventure. Comprising about a dozen stories and sketches which cover almost the whole span of the author's long and eventful life, the book is truly autobiographical, and brings to life for the reader an image of the author more vivid than any that a longer, more conventional autobiography or biography could ever do.

And what a loveable image it is!

Jim Corbett must have been a remarkable man; though a big-game hunter, he was a real lover of nature in all its manifestations; a man courageous and yet intensely human. These and other human qualities in a high order are well brought out in the stories of this book. Jim Corbett was also a wonderful storyteller, and his style is simple yet idiomatic. For this reason, I think that *My India* should be prescribed as a rapid reader for matriculation or intermediate students. It will tell them what qualities go to make a man. It may also give them a taste for outdoor life and nature which they woefully lack. They will also know that there are certain Englishmen who loved India as their own country.

—Letter to the Editor by S.A. Bashir, Ahmedabad,
The Times of India, 30 March 1960.

Dear Miss Corbett,
You will be pleased to see a copy of the letter which appears in this morning's *Times of India*. I have no idea who this S.A. Bashir is. An educational edition of *My India* has been issued, and has been used in some South Indian universities. Let us hope it will be even more widely read.

—Roy E. Hawkins' letter to Margaret Corbett,
30 March 1960

Dear Mr Hawkins,
Thank you very much for so kindly sending me a copy of the letter written by S.A. Bashir, which appeared in the *Times of India*...

The appreciation of Indians of Jim's work is very touching. I have always felt that his books, especially *My India*, reveal his character so vividly, and he has—quite unconsciously—written his very self into them, so that they are, in a sense, autobiographical...

—Margaret Corbett's letter to Roy E. Hawkins from
Nyeri, Kenya, 4 April 1960

The Tigress and the Kid Incident[‡]

Dear Mr Hawkins,

I must thank you for affording me the opportunity to read Corbett's *My India* Chapters I–V. Needless to say, I enjoyed every story, and found them well-written in his inimitable style. To city-dwellers, it presents a very true picture of the remote countryside and its mode of life with which we are not all familiar. I have found the same type of people in my jungle wanderings—simple, honest, trustworthy folk and who are very superstitious, and really appreciate even the smallest kindness, but not always reliable in a tight spot, for example, when facing a wounded tiger, or the like.

The incident of the tiger and the kid is remarkable and almost unbelievable although I have to admit that a tiger is very particular about his beef and is known to choose the fattest kine in a herd. This might be the explanation for the tigress' behaviour—the morsel was dainty but not enough to satisfy her appetite.

The incident of the tiger pinning Har Singh to the tree in Chapter 2 without attacking him with tooth and claw is equally remarkable. Apparently, it wanted to teach him a very severe lesson, and I have no doubt it succeeded. The scratch to his stomach was purely accidental, and could have been caused by one of the hind feet as they were lifted to maintain its balance.

‡ In Chapter 5 ('The Law of the Jungles') of *My India*, Corbett describes the 'nose to nose' meeting of a 'stalking' tigress and 'a month old kid'. The kid sees the tigress and begins bleating whereupon the tigress walks right up to the kid. When the tigress gets to within a few yards, the kid innocently moves up to her, stretches out its neck, and lifts its head to smell her. However, after a few 'tense' moments, the tigress turns around and walks off into the direction from which she has come.

The book, if published, should prove very popular and add to Corbett's reputation as a writer.

—Ernst D' Brass [Oxford University Press, Madras]
letter to Roy E. Hawkins, 18 October 1948

My dear D' Brass,

I am so glad to hear you enjoyed Corbett's new stories. I fear you have hit upon the right explanation for the tigress' gentlemanly behaviour towards the kid! I feel sure the explanation must have occurred to Corbett too ... so I think I will send him an extract from your note and see what he says ...

—Roy E. Hawkins' letter to Earnest D' Brass
[Oxford University Press, Madras], 20 October 1948

My dear Hawkins,

... I was very interested to read D' Brass' [note] on the tigress and the kid incident. He would have thought the incident more remarkable and unbelievable if I had mentioned that the tigress had three small cubs in a thick patch of lantana nearby, and immediately after leaving the kid, she shooed me out of the jungle, and would have killed me if I had not done what she wanted me to do, for I was unarmed. The point I wanted to make was that in the jungles, there is consideration for the weak and the helpless; otherwise there would have been no way of accounting for the safe return of the two children.§ To me

§ Two-year-old Putali and three-year-old Punwa were lost in the forest around midday on a Friday and were found by herdsman around 5 p.m., on the following Monday—'a matter of seventy-seven hours'. The children were found sleeping, clasped in each other's arms, weak and hungry, but spared the perils of the jungle. The episode is recounted in the chapter 'The Law of the Jungles' in Corbett's My India. See section titled 'The Missing Children' below.

incidents of this kind are quite natural, but I can quite understand that to others they appear unbelievable...

—Jim Corbett's letter to Roy E. Hawkins,

6 November 1948

My dear Miss Corbett,

... I expect you have heard that the book is getting a very good reception from the press in America. The USIS Wireless Bulletin today is largely made up of a series of quotations from Rupert Trumbal's review in *The New York Times*. He says, among other things, 'most people who know this country, and love it, will say that Jim Corbett's *My India* is their India'. Certainly this book is having a better start than *The Leopard*.

—Roy E. Hawkins' letter to Margaret Corbett,

27 May 1952

My dear Corbett,

... Excellent reviews of *My India* continue to appear in the Indian and English papers, and I hope you are glad to be compared to Rudyard Kipling in the power to transport your readers to India. Our sales here of the book were 1186 for the first three months, which I can assure you is exceedingly good in these times for any book which is not a textbook.

—Roy E. Hawkins' letter to Jim Corbett,

1 August 1952

The Missing Children

Dear Sir,

I read a brief condensation by *Reader's Digest* of your publication *My India* by Jim Corbett. The moving episode there about Putali and

Punwa, two children, the sole worldly possessions of their parents, was highly appreciated, and I wrote to *Reader's Digest*, 25 Berkeley Sq. W expressing my appreciation, and added that Ceylon being so close to India, it would be worthwhile if the whereabouts of these two children, or at least the post town, etc. where they live now be known.

As the author Mr Jim Corbett died in 1955, they (*Digest*) wrote to me that they could not help me, but suggested that OUP will certainly be able to detect the children through the Indian Branch.

I shall be grateful if you could oblige me with this information and whether the complete book is available in Ceylon. The *Digest* letter was dated 25 March 1959, signed by Elizabeth Scott.

—Dr D.A. Ranasinha's letter [from Ratnagiri, Batuwatte, Ragama, Ceylon] to Oxford University Press, London, 26 April 1959

I attach a letter from Dr D.A. Ranasinha of Ceylon, which we have acknowledged.

I wonder whether you could help him trace the two children, Putali and Punwa, mentioned in *My India*.

—Letter to Oxford University Press, Bombay, from Oxford University Press, London, 8 May 1959

Dear Dr Ranasinha,

Your letter asking for information about Punwa and Putali has been forwarded to us here in Bombay. I think it is extremely unlikely that we can find these two people for you as Jim Corbett was, in *My India*, writing about his experiences in his younger days, and the incident referred to in the extract you have read may have occurred as long ago as 1900. It is therefore likely that these 'babes in the wood' are now separated, in middle age, and perhaps unknown in Kaladhungi.

Even if we can trace them, they will probably be very unlike the pitiable children described by Corbett. Nevertheless, I am making an attempt to locate them through the authorities in Naini Tal.

—R.A.S. Melluish's [Assistant Manager, Oxford University Press, Bombay] letter to Dr D.A. Ranasinha, 'Ratnagiri', Batuwatte, Ragama, Ceylon, 13 May 1959

Dear Sir,

In 1952 we published a book called *My India* by Colonel Jim Corbett, who spent many years living in Naini Tal. In it there is a story about two children in Kaladhungi who got lost in the forest, a boy named Punwa and a girl Putali. Their father was called Harkwa and their mother Kunthi. The story of the infants' survival after some days alone and helpless in the jungle full of wild beasts has moved a philanthropic gentleman in Ceylon to write to us, the publishers, to ask if we will try to discover where Punwa and Putali are now.

I should be very surprised if we found these people, particularly as there is no indication in the book as to when Corbett knew them. It may have been fifty years ago. Moreover, he may have changed their names while writing the book although this is unlikely since he describes the incidents related as being true and unembellished.

However, I think you may be able to help if anyone can, and so I write to ask whether you would be kind enough to make some enquiries in the neighbourhood as to their present whereabouts. Many thanks.

—R.A.S. Melluish's [Assistant Manager, Oxford University Press, Bombay] letter to the Forest Inspector, Kaladhungi, Naini Tal, 20 May 1959

'Shooting' Tigers

Corbett and the Camera*

I think all sportsmen who have had the opportunity of indulging in the twin sport of shooting tigers with a rifle, and shooting them with a camera, are agreed that the difference between these two forms of sport is as great, if not greater than the killing of a tank fish with a fixed rod and a fid of paste, and the taking of a two-pound trout on a light tackle on a fly of ounes in a mountain stream.

From the difference in cost between shooting with a rifle and a camera and the added skill and patience needed, the taking of a good photograph which can be shared with one's friends, and the sporting public at large, gives far more pleasure than the acquisition of a trophy which is only of one person's interest and which, at best,

---

* A version of this essay was previously published in *Jim Corbett's India: Stories Selected by R.E. Hawkins* (New Delhi: Oxford University Press, 1978).

endures only for a few years. As an illustration, I would cite Fred Champion.† If Champion had shot his tigers, he would not have got one-tenth of the pleasure he got by photographing them, and where in one case he would have had a trophy to hang on his walls for only personal interest, he has with his photographs given pleasure to lovers of wildlife all over the world.

It was looking at Champion's photographs in his book *Sunlight and Shadow* that first gave me the idea of taking tiger photographs. His photographs were taken by flashlight, and I decided to go one better and try and take tiger photographs with a cinema camera in daylight. The gift by a very generous sporting friend of a 16-mm camera put the appliance I needed into my hands, and the 'freedom of the forests', which I enjoy, enabled me to roam over a large field. For ten years, I stalked through many hundreds of miles of tiger country, at times being seen off by tigers who resented my approaching their kills and, at other times, being shooed out of the jungle by tigresses who objected to my going too near their cubs. During this time, I learnt a little about the habits and ways of tigers, and though I saw tigers on several hundred occasions, I did not succeed in getting a satisfactory picture. I exposed film on quite a number of occasions, but the results owing to overexposure, underexposure, obstruction of grass or leaves between the lens and the object, or error of temperature in the developing solution, were not satisfactory.

† Frederick Walter Champion (1893–1970) was an English forester who worked in British India and East Africa, and became famous in the 1920s as the first wildlife photographer and conservationist. Using flashlights, he obtained dozens of remarkable night-time photographs, which are among the first of wild tigers, leopards, sloth bears and dholes, and other wildlife. He recognized that with good photographs of tigers, it was possible to tell individuals apart by their different stripe patterns.

Finally, in 1938, I decided to devote the whole winter in making one last attempt to get a good picture. The first consideration was to find a site for my picture, and I finally selected an open ravine 50 yards wide, with a minimum stream flowing through it, and flanked on either side with dense tree and scrub jungle. To deaden the sound of my camera when taking pictures at a short range, I diverted the stream, and made two or three waterfalls a few inches high. I then cast around for my tigers and having located seven, I attracted them by slow degrees to the spot I had prepared for their reception. One of these tigers, for some reason unknown to me, left the day after I took a picture of it, but I managed to keep the others together and exposed a 1000 feet of film on them. Unfortunately, it was one of the wettest winters we have ever had, and several hundred feet of the film were spoilt either through moisture on the lens, or the packing of the film inside the camera through hurried and careless threading of the film, and through underexposure.

But even so, I have got approximately 600 feet of film of which I am excessively proud for they show six full-grown tigers—four males and two females—taken at ranges varying from 10 to 60 feet in daylight and in their natural surroundings. The whole proceeding, from start to finish, took four and a half months and during the whole of that time, not one of the tigers ever saw me. The tigers were stalked in the dark—the heavy winter dew made this possible—and were filmed as light and opportunity offered.

The enlargements made from 16-mm films are not as clear as they would have been if they had been taken with a still camera, but the pictures when projected are clear...

Wildlife in the Village
An Environmental Appeal*

It was a small village of some sixteen ploughs differing in no respect
from hundreds of similar villages scattered throughout the length of
the tract along the Bhabar. Originally, the village had been surrounded
by tree jungle intercepted with grass, and in this virgin jungle lived

* This essay was previously published as 'Wild Life in the Village: an Appeal'
in *Jim Corbett's India: Stories Selected by R.E. Hawkins* (New Delhi: Oxford
University Press, 1978).

all the numerous denizens of the wild. To protect their crops, the villagers erected thorn fences around their fields. As an additional safeguard, a member of the depressed class was encouraged to settle in the village whose duty it was to watch the crops at night, and see they were not damaged by stray cattle or wild animals. Owing to the abundance of game, tigers did not interfere with the village cattle, and I cannot remember a single case of a cow or bullock having been killed by a tiger. In the course of time, a great change took place, not only in the villagers themselves but also in the jungle surrounding the village. Hindus, who formerly looked upon the taking of life as against their religious principles, were now clamouring for gun licences, and were competing with each other in the indiscriminate slaughter of game. As profits from the sale of game increased, field work was neglected and land began to go out of cultivation.

Simultaneously, lantana, introduced into Haldwani as a pot plant, started to kill out the grass and *basonta* until the village was surrounded with a dense growth of this obnoxious weed. The Government now stepped in and, at great expense, built a pucca wall all round the village. The building of this wall freed the villagers from the necessity of erecting fences and watching their crops, and gave them more time to devote to the killing of the game. This heavy and unrestricted shooting of deer had the inevitable consequence of disturbing the balance in nature with the result that tigers and leopards that had hitherto lived on game were now forced to live on the village cattle. One morning in May of the present year, I arrived in the village and pitched my tent in a little clearing just outside the cultivated land. News of my arrival soon spread through the village and, in a short time, a dozen men were squatting in front of my tent. One and all had some tale to tell. A tiger had taken up its quarters in the lantana and, in the course of two years, had killed 150 head of cattle, and unless it was destroyed, the village would have to be abandoned.

While the men were pouring out their tale of woe, I observed a pair of vultures circling low over a narrow stretch of lantana running between the village men and the public road. The two vultures were soon joined by others; so, picking up a rifle, I set off to investigate. Progress through the lantana was difficult, but with the aid of a good hunting knife, a way was eventually cut and the remains of a horse killed the previous day found. There were plenty of pug marks around the kill, little of which remained, and it was easy to locate the tiger from his low continuous growling but impossible to see him in the dense cover. Returning to the road, which was only 40 yards round the kill and little used at this time of year, I concealed myself behind a bush in the hope that the tiger would follow me to see if I had left the locality, quite a natural thing for it to do. Half an hour later, the tiger walked out onto the road and gave me an easy shot as he stood facing me. That evening, after I had skinned the tiger—he was a very old animal and I took four old bullets and nine pellets of buck-shots out of him—I called the villagers together and made an appeal to them on behalf of the few remaining deer in the jungle. On the opposite side of the village from my camp, irrigation water had been allowed to flow into the jungle. Over this water, machans had been built in the trees and in these machans men sat through the heat of the day and all night long on moonlit nights, and shot down animals that came to drink. There was no other water within miles, and if a thirst-maddened animal avoided one machan, it fell victim to the man in the next. I told the villagers that God had given water free for all, and that it was a shameful thing for man to sit over the water God had provided and shoot His creatures when they came to drink. To do this was to lower themselves below a corpse-eating hyena, for even he, the lowest of all creation, did not lie in wait to kill defenceless animals while they were drinking. The men listened to me in silence and when I had done, said they had not looked at the matter in this light, and they promised that they would take down the machans they had erected and, in future, would not molest the animals that came to the vicinity of the village to drink. I stayed in the locality several weeks, taking bird and animal pictures, and am glad to say the men kept their promise. I believe that much of the slaughter of deer that is daily taking place throughout the length and breadth of the Bhabar and Tarai would cease if an appeal was made to the better feelings of men.

I do not exaggerate the damage that is being done to our fauna by shooting over water. Let me give you but one instance. An acquaintance of mine living in a village in the Bhabar adjoining mine, in one hot season, over one small pool of water shot, with a single-barrel muzzle-loading gun, sixty heads of cheetal and sambhar which he sold in a nearby bazaar at the rate of Rs 5 per cheetal and Rs10 per sambhar. It is no exaggeration to say that the banks of every little stream and every pool of water in the vicinity of Bhabar villages are soaked with the blood of animals that never took toll of a single blade of the villagers' crops. I assert without fear of contradiction that, for every shot fired on cultivated land from guns provided for crop protection, a hundred shots are fired in the jungle over water. Pigs and neelgai are the only wild animals that damage the crops in the Bhabar to any extent, and to keep them out of cultivated land, Government has expended lakhs of rupees in building pucca walls. It is asserted that, in recent years, tigers have increased. With this assertion I do not agree. It is a fact that more cattle are being killed every year, but this is not due to the tigers having increased. It is due to the balance of nature having been disturbed by the unrestricted slaughter to of game, and also to some extent it is due to tigers having been driven out of their natural haunts where they were seldom or never seen by man, or by the activities of the Forest Department.

A country's fauna is a sacred trust, and I appeal to you not to betray this trust. Shooting over water, shooting over salt-licks, natural and artificial, shooting birds in the close season and when roosting at night, encouraging permit-holders to shoot hinds, fencing off of large areas of forest and the extermination by the Forest Department of all game within these areas, making of unnecessary motor tracks through the forest and shooting from motor cars, absence of sanctuaries and the burning of forests by the Forest Department and by villagers at a time when the forests are full of young life are all combining to one end—the extermination of our fauna. If we do not bestir ourselves now, it will be to our discredit that the fauna of our province was exterminated in our generation and under our very eyes, while we looked on and never raised a finger to prevent it.

An Englishman in India

Mokameh Ghat*

...I will spend only one more April away from home. Leaving the question of discomfort of climate out of the question, I love the

* Corbett was appointed trans-shipment inspector with the Bengal and North-Western Railway (BNWR) in 1895 and was sent to Mokameh Ghat in Bihar on a salary of Rs 150 per month. He later became a contractor for the trans-shipment of goods across the Ganges at Mokameh Ghat. In all, he worked at Mokameh Ghat for twenty-two years. 'As for tiger hunting, he fitted that in here and there ...' (Martin Booth, 1990 [1986], *Carpet Sahib: A Life of Jim Corbett*, Oxford University Press, p. 77).

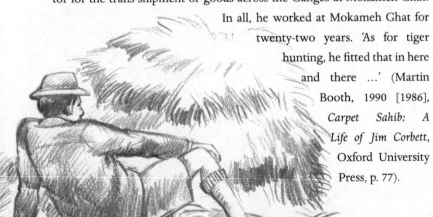

work here and will be sorry to give it up and sever my connection with all the men I have collected together; but leave it all I must some day and as there will be no necessity for my staying on after next year, it follows that next year will be the best time for me to leave, and that for many reasons. A leading barrister from Bankipur travelling up First Class from Calcutta a few days ago told one of our men there would be no European in Bengal in ten years. I quite agree with him.

Our Raj is trembling in the balance and as one can do no good, what sense is there in waiting to be buried in its ruins. By next year, I will have got all I want out of Mokameh Ghat, and though I will leave the place with many regrets, still it will be a relief to get away, especially as getting away for me means going home.

—Jim Corbett, 17 April 1914

Mokameh Ghat

I got a wire this morning to attend Chinsura Court in a railway case relating to a wagon of hides that fell into the river three years ago. Needless to say, I am not going; with the new ghat to be opened tomorrow and all the work I have in hand, I can't possibly leave, and further I don't know anything about the case as I was in Naini Tal when the accident happened. If the railway or the court forces me, I will demand to be heard on commission, as the court is over 200 miles from my place of residence.

I would love to take a run home for a few days, but it can't possibly be done. With the traffic as heavy as it is, and Ramsaran going to Bhagalpur, I will not be able to leave the station for a single day until I leave it for good. November I think will be as good a time as any for me to leave. With the difficulty there is now of getting labour and keeping it together, the contract is not now worth having, and if I can get anyone to take it away from me, I will gladly give it up. I do not consider that I am under any obligation to the railway. They have paid me just as they would have had to pay anyone else, and I have given then the best value I could for the money, so we are quits all round. One thing I am quite sure of, and that is that the railway will not get anyone to run Mokameh Ghat on Rs 250.... True, I have the contract, but that, to my way of thinking, increases my value a hundred per cent. Our big men on the railway are very good chaps, but they are not businessmen.

—Jim Corbett, 19 July 1914

My dear Brander,

Neither you nor I have spent anything on postage stamps recently, you because you have other things to think of, and I because I have been packing, and am too close to the horrors.

If the leaders at your end and mine co-opted the devil when drawing up their plan for the rivers in India to run with blood, they can today congratulate themselves on having planned with great success, for never in any part of the world has there been greater slaughter, with as much brutality, as India is witnessing today. And the end is not yet, for disease and famine have to take their toll, as have the frontier tribes, who in their turn will be followed by the Russians. And all this misery has been brought about by the leaders at your end, trying to earn a little cheap popularity for themselves, and by the leaders at my end being vain enough to think that they could break a dam and stop the rush of water by merely raising a hand. When all the pent-up water, fouled with blood, has seeped into the land, the Russians will quietly walk in, and no one in this stricken land will raise a protest. Yes, the leaders and the devil can indeed congratulate themselves on having done a very thorough job. Millions of people old and young are on the move by road and rail, and yesterday we were told over the wireless that between the

18th and 23rd of September, seven refugee trains had been attacked, and that out of one train alone, a thousand dead bodies had been removed. And this is not war; it is India, the real India, who for two hundred years has lived in peace and happiness under the rule of a handful of men, enjoying the freedom that has been thrust on her by a parcel of fools. The India that you and I loved has been sacrificed on the altars of ambition and greed, and has gone forever. It was my intention to try and regain my health in Kenya, and then come back and try and better the lot of the people among whom I have spent so many happy years—the whole of my life in fact—but that intention must now be abandoned, for it is too distressing to stand by and see my friends flying to each other's throats for no other reason than they wear different headgear.

★ ★ ★

You will be seeing Hawkins, for he has gone home, via the USA on long leave. The proofs of the new book were to have been sent to me weeks ago, but they have not arrived yet; and this is not surprising for all public services are disorganized, and it is quite possible that, in order to catch our boat next month, we will have to go first to Calcutta and travel by train from there to Bombay. Our luggage, including my guns, rods, and the man-eater skins will go via Jhansi— provided the trains over that section are running—and will have to take their chance, which is a poor one.

I have suggested to Hawkins employing Literary Agents in London and New York to look after the interests of *Man-Eaters* and *Rudraprayag.* Owing to the distance, I cannot keep in touch with these two places. ... An agent would keep me informed...

—Jim Corbett's letter to Brander, from Gurney House,

Naini Tal, India, 25 September 1947

Life in Kenya

[In 1947, India became independent and almost all the British people left India. Jim Corbett and his sister Maggie also left in November 1947, and settled in Kenya. They stayed at the Paxtu Cottage where Lord Baden-Powell* spent his last years. Jim had visited East Africa before, hunting lions with Percy Wyndham with whom he jointly

* Lord Baden-Powell was a lieutenant-general in the British Army, serving from 1876 until 1910 in India and Africa. He was also a writer, and founder of the Boy Scouts Movement. He wrote *Scouting for Boys* (1908) for youth readership. During writing, he tested his ideas through a camping trip on Brownsea Island with the local Boys' Brigade and sons of his friends that began on 1 August 1907, which is now seen as the beginning of Scouting. He lived his last years in Nyeri, Kenya, where he died and was buried in 1941.

owned a coffee farm—Kikafu Estate—on the slopes of Kilimanjaro, near the town Moshi in Tanganyika. However, throughout his stay in Kenya, his heart was in the Kumaon where he had lived his best years. He relived all his experiences in the India he loved as he wrote *My India* (1952), *Jungle Lore* (1953), *Temple Tiger and More Man-eaters* (1954). His last work, *Tree Tops* (1955), was an account of his escorting the Princess Elizabeth to a game lodge built on a ficus tree. While she was there her father, King George V, died in his sleep in Sandringham. Immediately after his death, the princess was declared queen, that is, Queen Elizabeth II. —Editor]

... Yes, I am trying to get out to Kenya. I served in low-lying jungles both here and in Burma during the war and collected every known type of malaria and tick typhus. Three times I have—much to the surprise of doctors and nurses—walked out of hospitals, but I have been told very definitely that if there is ever a fourth time, I will be carried out feet first. So I am going to Kenya to try and regain my health, for there are a thousand things I want to do before I finally turn up my toes, among them, a visit to the USA. I also want to bring out a third book which will take some time to write, for in it I will tell my friends all that I have learnt of jungle lore in a life spent in the jungles.

—Jim Corbett's letter to Philip Vaudrin, Oxford
University Press, New York, 16 October 1947

My dear Hawkins,

... The next time you take leave, you must go home via Kenya, and on our trout rivers you will forget all your troubles. Kenya today is full of people who are trying to do just that—forget their troubles and make new homes for themselves. I don't know if I told you that we are living at the Outspan Hotel in the cottage in which Baden-Powell spent the last years of his life. In this cottage, in which we are all very comfortable, I will write *My India* while the hotel builds a new cottage for us in which we will be more private, and will have more accommodation for our friends—when they come to us to forget all their troubles...

—Jim Corbett's letter to Roy E. Hawkins from
Nyeri, Kenya, 23 July 1948

My dear Hawkins,

... You will be interested to hear that four of us from India: Ibbotson, Friar Tuck, Brett, and I, took over, a year ago, a company (Safariland) started early in the century to cater for sportsmen coming to Kenya. During the Berlin airlift, the company feared that war was coming— they had a bad time during Hitler's war—and they sold out to us in a hurry. (My only object in joining the company was to discourage killing and encourage photography.) From the day we took over, the company has been booming, and we have more applicants than we can deal with. People come to us from all parts of the world, and this necessitates our employing men who know a number of languages. We have a fleet of cars and lorries—we are permitted to purchase all the transport we need—hundreds of tents and tent equipment, and we employ twenty white hunters, and we employ a staff of five Europeans. In addition to several parties in the field, we are handling the Metro-Golden-Mayer party of fifty-three who arrived three weeks ago from Hollywood to make a film which will be released under the name *King Solomon's Mines*. This party will be with us for thirteen weeks, and before they leave, another party of fifty Americans will arrive by air to take pictures of wildlife. Yesterday, I was asked by the Director of Information whether I would help the Hollywood party by making animal calls for their film. He also asked me if I would sell the coloured films I recently took of elephants in Uganda. My throat is now too old to make animal calls, and never having made money from my pictures, I am not going to start now. However, if after attending the cinema show I am giving here on the 31st of this month, the Hollywood people think my pictures will be of use to them, I will give them to them, as a small return for all the American Branch of Oxford University Press has done for me. Unfortunately, the Americans do not appreciate free gifts; [but] that can't be helped...

—Jim Corbett's letter to Roy E. Hawkins from
Nyeri, Kenya, 22 October 1949

My dear Corbett,

... Your Safari enterprise must be a good dollar earner, and I have no doubt it keeps you busy. If the film director persuaded you to appear in *King Solomon's Mines*, I hope you will let me know. I imagine you are immortalised in many a cine-camera film now...

—Roy E. Hawkins' letter to Jim Corbett from
Nyeri, Kenya, 7 November 1949

My dear Cumberlege,

... The Prime Minister of the United Provinces wants me to go back to my home in Naini Tal and if, later on, I can see my way to spend a few months each year there, I will try and get a fresh lot of illustrations for further editions of our books... I was unable to get a picture of 'The Queen of the Village' [in *My India*]. She, and other high-caste women, while anxious to help me in every way they can, are unable to overcome their objection to being photographed.

... I have written about half of *Jungle Lore* and I am not dissatisfied with what I have written, for even if I have murdered the King's English, the book will give sportsmen information that no book has ever yet given.... If I could spend another winter in an Indian jungle, with a good camera, I could support many of the statements with photographs; and, failing photographs, I will have to rely on word pictures which are not satisfactory. Hawkins suggested that if the book [*Jungle Lore*] was too long, it could be brought out in two volumes. However, this is a matter you can decide when you have seen the MS. *Jungle Lore* will be my last book—not because I have run dry—and I am writing it with great pleasure for I am living over again my happiest days, and I want to share those happy days with the many friends my books have made for me. These friends accepted a total stranger at his face value, and I am very grateful to them.

—Jim Corbett's letter to Geoffrey J. Cumberlege,

25 January 1951

My dear Corbett,

… Coming up in the train from home this morning, I read the *TLS* review and decided that I would send it off to you. Within an hour or two, there arrived your letter of the 24th offering us the .275 rifle presented to you by Sir John Hewell. Naturally we should love to have this, and we shall make full use of it, not for shooting refractory authors but for display with your books as opportunities occur! Will there be any difficulty about getting the rifle sent over? If you will let me know when it has been shipped, I shall be glad as there may be certain formalities with the customs to be got over.

—Extract from Geoffrey J. Cumberlege's letter to

Jim Corbett, 30 October 1953

My dear Cumberlege,

I am so glad to learn from your letter of 9 November that our new book is going so well. A second edition, within a month, of the fifth book while the other four are still selling well, is an achievement of which we can be justifiably proud. The dock strike has unfortunately delayed the dispatch of the book from England, and anxiety is being felt in Kenya that it will not arrive in time for the Christmas market.

I am very sorry for the mistake about the copies I wanted sent to friends, and the copies I wanted for myself. Under cover of my letter of 30 July, I sent a list of twelve names and requested that a copy of *Temple Tiger* be sent to the addresses given, and the cost debited to my account. Later, I added one more name to the list, Tweedie's. Then again, on 15 September, I asked for the remaining five author's copies to be sent to me, together with six additional copies which were to be debited to me. So actually I am in your debt for nineteen copies, 12+1+6.

There is no improvement in the situation here; however, it could be worse, and grousing won't make it any better. We will enjoy the peace and quiet of England when we take our holiday next year. 'Next year' sounds a long way off but the time will soon pass, for we have lots to do in the house and in the garden, and we can still see well enough to do a little reading and writing. I have had to give up photography, but hope to be able to take it up again after my eyes have been operated on in London. Eye operations out here are not always a success, and we can't afford to take risks.

The sun is shining after a night of rain; the jacarandas are in full bloom, and our garden is a blaze of colour and—a few miles away—bombs are bursting. Human beings are never happy unless they are fighting, or going on strike over small matters that could be settled over a bottle of beer.

Our kindest regards to both of you.

—Jim Corbett's letter to Geoffrey J. Cumberlege,
17 November 1954

SECTION TWO

Corbett and his Audience
(From the OUP Archives)

'The Artlessness of his Art'

In his Introduction to Jim Corbett's last book, *Tree Tops*—a model, let it be said, of what a biographical introduction should be—Lord Hailey wonders 'how far the picture formed of him by his readers differs from that which will live in the memory of his friends'. So far as it is possible to give an answer to that interesting speculation, the correct one would seem to be: 'Very widely indeed'. Of the millions of people throughout the world who have derived such pleasure from his books, the majority probably have visualized the author as a tough, brisk figure with the terse directness one would instinctively associate with a lifetime of giving orders. Anyone with his utter fearlessness must be mentally tough, the argument would run, just as anyone who thought nothing of a 28 mile march in pouring rain over precipitous mountain tracks must be physically tough; similarly, a man specially selected to train troops in jungle fighting in the Second World War, and more particularly one who could recruit and control for years the large Indian labour force he employed as a contractor to the Railway Department, must be gifted with exceptional powers of command. The process of deduction is logical enough. Yet, to nine people out of ten, it would convey an entirely wrong impression of a gentle, lovable personality. It may be worthwhile, therefore, trying to give a clearer picture of what the man was really like, who is famous the world over as an outstanding storyteller and—what meant much more to him—was reverenced and loved throughout Kumaon and its neighbouring districts.

Fortunately, when leaving India at the end of 1947, there was no need for difficult heart searchings as to what new country would suit him and his sister best as a place of residence. From previous visits, Jim knew and liked East Africa. He had relatives in Kenya, and friends of the old Indian days. So, to Kenya they came, and it is typical of them both that they transferred to their tenants in Kaladhungi as a free gift the ownership of their property there.

Soon after their arrival in Kenya, they went to live in the pleasant cottage in the Outspan Hotel at Nyeri in which Lord Baden-Powell spent the last years of his life. Except for the distressing accident when Maggie slipped and broke a thigh, the next five years were a time of unalloyed content. Owing largely to her magnificent courage, her recovery was amazingly rapid and complete. Long before the most optimistic thought it possible, she was back in the cottage with her beloved brother. Theirs was a devoted and extraordinarily happy companionship; and if, to use her own words, he was 'a wonderful brother' to her, she was equally a wonderful sister to him.

The Man Mau outbreak brought to all Nyeri residents inconveniences, anxieties, and periodical alarms; but living as they were in a large hotel within the township limits, the Corbetts did not find the quiet routine of their lives seriously affected. It was during the time the trouble was at its height in the district that *The Temple Tiger* was written. Readers of that volume may be interested to know that it took a lot of persuasion, or if his own plaintive description is preferred, 'bullying', to get Jim Corbett to write it. He had at the time, ideas in his head for two other books. One of them was *Tree Tops*, which he finished less than a fortnight before his death. The other, at that time no more than very vaguely planned, was to have been rather on the lines of *Jungle Lore*, with the special object of urging on the younger generation his faith, born of his own experience that, in the long run, an intelligent study of nature offers greater rewards than mere killing can ever do. The public must be tired of his man-eaters, he protested. He would write the other two books first; and perhaps, afterwards, the spirit might move him to tell of the tiger that took all the honours of their encounters at Dabhidhura, of the Panar leopard credited with four hundred human kills in days when records were possibly not as complete as they were later, and of the epic hunt that ended in the deaths of the Talla Des tigress and her two cubs. But the 'bully' who had listened enthralled to *The Temple Tiger* stories, told by word of mouth, was inexorable, and Jim finally submitted with good grace. Once started, he found the going easy, as he afterwards confessed, and the result was a collection of tales, which not a few of his readers will rank among the best he wrote.

Man-Eaters of Kumaon and the account of the arduous months he spent on the trail of the Rudraprayag leopard were written in India. His other four books were produced in the Outspan cottage, where anyone paying a morning call would have been almost certain to find him at his desk in a corner of the pleasant sitting-room, tapping away with one finger at his ancient typewriter. Not only did he scrap and retype any page that had even one mistake on it, but he typed four copies of all his books, one for each of his publishers in England, America, and India, and one home copy, till very often that one finger of his was sore and bleeding. If not actually typing, he generally seemed to be wrestling with a deplorable red and black ribbon, trying to coax a few more words out of it before he was forced to do the hated task of putting in a new one.

It was something of a marvel that he managed to write his books at all, let alone finish them as quickly as he did, in face of the demands made on his time by his own correspondence and the number of people coming to see him. His usual working hours were between breakfast and lunch and, in the evenings, he generally went through the day's output, and if the quantity justified it, with his sister, to whose advice and criticism he always acknowledged he owed so much. Incidentally, she was, like him, blessed with a wonderful memory. If a name or date did escape him, it was invariably a case of 'I'll ask Maggie'. And, it was rarely that Maggie failed to provide the answer. But, there were so many mornings when little progress was possible. It did not occur to him to shut himself away from the interruptions that would shatter the train of thought of the less imperturbable, and leave them with the exasperating task of getting the run of the story into action again. He had a priceless gift of being able to stop in the middle of a sentence, to welcome and chat with perhaps a complete stranger and then, after his visitor had gone, of picking up without hesitation the thread of his narrative exactly where it had been broken off. Not many authors could do their work on those syncopated lines.

He took his time over selecting his subject matter from the immense stores of material provided by his long experience, acute observation, and the patient study of everything that went into the making of that part of the world in which it had pleased Providence to cast his lot. Once his book was planned, the actual writing of it was a relatively simple matter. He was fortunate in being spared the pangs of literary travail. He was never afflicted, for instance, with that miserable sense of frustration that descends upon the novelist when the well of inspiration runs dry; for Jim Corbett's stories owed nothing to fiction nor to anything other than fact; they were unadorned records of actual experiences. His photographic memory enabled him to recall in minute detail particular events of many years before, and he related each incident precisely as he remembered it. He never tampered with truth for the sake of effect. If he was not satisfied as to the accuracy of some detail, he would never include it for the purpose of making it picturesque or adding excitement to the tale. The part of the picture he did consistently under-colour was that which would have shown in proper perspective the mental strain and physical hardships he endured. Only once in his books—in the story of the Talla Des man-eater—did he make more than a casual reference to his bodily ills, and then only because his sufferings played an essential part in the narrative. For the rest, the reader's imagination had to fill in the record of sickness, exhaustion, and nerve-racking tension.

Jim Corbett provided a flat contradiction of Pope's aphorism that 'true ease in writing comes from art, not chance'. Writing came easily to him for the very reason that it came naturally. Had he lived to double the number of his books, the style of the last would have been as devoid of artificiality as that of the first. The great merit of his art lay in its artlessness. He wrote just as he lived and thought, with a complete lack of self-consciousness and affectation. He had not, nor could he ever have acquired, the airs and graces that can be cultivated by constant practice. All that mattered to him was that the tale he was telling should be true; and when one is dealing in objective verities, there is little room for meretricious embellishment.

He used to chuckle over the tributes paid in reviews of his books to his 'skill' as an author. He had no literary skill, he maintained; all he could do was to put on paper an unvarnished account of experiences and observances. It is perfectly true that his stories were essentially reportorial in that they were factual records of incidents as they happened; but it was magnificent reporting, all the more vivid for the unaffected simplicity with which it was done.

There was an engaging naiveté in his reactions to the enthusiastic reception the world gave to his books. He could understand that they might have some appeal for people interested in big-game shooting or in the jungle life of India; but when he began to receive warmly congratulatory letters from such unlikely sources as, for instance, elderly ladies living sheltered lives in small American country towns, to whom his subjects would not normally be expected to appeal, he was at first slightly bewildered. His unassuming mind did not find it easy to appreciate the fact that the manner of telling a tale could make it acceptable to many to whom the theme, if differently treated, might be distasteful. Later, when he became more accustomed to these gratifying manifestations of goodwill, he still tended at heart to regard them more as revelations of human kindness than as authentic tributes to his own talent. There was no false modesty in this depreciation of his brilliant gift of story-telling; he was genuinely astonished at the worldwide renown *Man-Eaters of Kumaon* brought him. He was very pleased, highly amazed, and slightly awed.

Fame made not the least difference to Jim Corbett; he remained just the same quiet, unpretentious person he had always been, untainted by any trace of conceit. He continued to live the same retiring life, occupying himself with his writing, which now included tapping out answers to all the letters of his formidable fan mail, and with his cameras.

Although his sense of duty to the hill-folk of Kumaon had led him to continue his pursuit of man-eaters long after others with less than his determination and extraordinary powers of endurance would have found the task beyond them, he had no regrets when the time came to lay aside his rifle with a clear conscience. He had never been a bloodthirsty man, who slew for slaughter's sake. In fact, if it were possible to arrive at a reasonable estimate of the number of creatures he had killed during his life, the figures would be surprisingly small, especially when the opportunities he had been given are considered. Even in the case of man-eaters, there was little satisfaction in the actual killing of animals on which he would, so to speak, have preferred to pass a sentence of 'guilty but insane'. They had to be shot, of course, for the protection of all those villagers who looked on him as their one infallible saviour; but at the back of his mind there was the thought that the man-eater was an abnormal specimen whose destruction, though necessary, gave occasion for some compunction. He was glad, therefore, when he could feel without reservation that he had done all he could, and that to younger men would pass the duty of answering the appeals for aid to which he had responded for so long with selfless generosity.

Kenya offered ample scope for the nature-photography which for years had increasingly absorbed his interest. Tree Tops was easily accessible. Still nearer at hand, some 3 miles from his door, elephants were often to be seen on, or only just off, one of the main roads out of Nyeri, at that time of the year when the heavy mists and slippery ground of the Long Rains brought them down from the higher forests of the Aberdare Mountains. He took some beautiful pictures of one big herd before several of its members were shot in the interest of public safety.

Further afield, there were the national parks and the national reserves, all of them affording, in greater or less measure, opportunities for the use of his cine-camera.

Not the least charming recollection of one's time in Nyeri is the memory of the Corbetts with the birds of their garden; and certainly no sketch of their lives during that period would be complete without some reference to their relations with their feathered companions.

One of the first things they did, on their arrival in the cottage, was to set about restoring the contacts Lord Baden-Powell had established when he lived there. Preliminary acquaintanceship soon ripened into confiding friendship, and friendship into hereditary intimacy, with succeeding generations bringing their newlyfledged young for personal introduction to the unfailing supplies of cake to be eaten from the hands offering it, or of the millet scattered around the fountain at the bottom of the steps leading up from the garden. When the weather permitted morning coffee on the veranda, the function was invariably attended by some hundreds of birds of upwards of a dozen species.

To the very end of his life, Jim Corbett carried his years lightly. When he was close on eighty, his tall lance-straight figure, with the sinewy spareness that recalled the exceptional physical powers he possessed in earlier days, would have done credit to a much younger man. There was abundant character apparent in the strongly-moulded face with the startlingly vivid, deep-blue eyes, set in a network of humorous wrinkles. At the same time, for all its strength, the face conveyed an abiding impression of gentle kindliness which was entirely in keeping with the man's character. He hated discord, and would go to any reasonable lengths to avoid becoming involved in controversy. There was no question of weakness in his ability to brook with equanimity words and actions that would have aroused open resentment in others less even-tempered than himself. His tolerance could always make allowances for the other person's point of view, however crotchety it might be, and though he might disagree or possibly deplore, it was very seldom that he was prepared to condemn outright. It is typical of his charitable outlook that neither in speaking or writing of man-eaters, even scourges as terrible as the Champawat tigress or the Panar leopard, would he employ synonyms like 'brute' or 'beast'. They were, in his view, victims of circumstances and, as such, were entitled to some degree of sympathetic understanding. Similarly, he refused to sit in harsh judgment on his fellow men just as firmly as he would decline to discuss them unless he had something good to say of them.

Jim Corbett was never a wealthy man. In his younger days, his abstemious mode of living enabled him to meet all necessary demands on his purse, and leave just enough over for indulging his love of jungle sport so far as his limited leisure permitted. It took years of hard work to build up the modest competence on which he retired to devote much of his time to the still more exacting occupation of dealing with the succession of man-eaters that terrorized Kumaon—an occupation, be it remembered, undertaken in the true spirit of service which looks for no reward. After his arrival in Kenya, the royalties from his books began to bring in an increasing, though not superabundant, addition to his income. But, if his means at no time approached opulence, he was passing rich in his friends; and a very catholic company they were, ranging from Viceroys and Governors of Provinces down to the humble cultivator tilling his fractional holding on a Himalayan hillside. The simplicity of his own character enabled him to meet prince or peasant on equal terms of unassuming ease; he was one of those rare beings who 'can walk with kings nor lose the common touch'.

The end of his full and happy life came with a merciful suddenness. He died as he had lived, thinking of others.

The Man Revealed
Corbett in his Writings

For a life of Jim Corbett we must read his six books. His autobiography is scattered throughout these pages. As one would expect from a modest man, the self-portrait is uneven, parts are clear while the rest faint or not drawn at all.... This is, perhaps, the occasion to fill in briefly some of the details. The task has been made easy and pleasant through the help and generosity of his devoted sister Maggie who has provided the writer with material and given him many happy hours of talk about her brother. With him she spent almost her entire life.

Colonel Edward James Corbett, to give him his full title, was born on 25 July 1875 at Naini Tal, a hill station of northern India. He was the eighth child of Christopher and Mary Jane Corbett who was the widow of Charles Doyle. His mother had been married to Doyle when she was fourteen, and bore him two sons and two daughters. One of these daughters died in infancy. They lived in Agra, and when the 'mutiny' broke out, she and the children were sent to live in the

Fort while Charles Doyle was fighting. There she suffered much. Her husband was killed and, at twenty-one, she was left a widow with very little to support herself and the three children. Not long after, she married Christopher Corbett, and by him she had six sons and three daughters. The last three of that family were Maggie, then Jim, and the youngest Archie. He and Jim were devoted friends, but he died at the age of twenty.

Christopher was a widower, and with him there came two sons and a daughter. The mother, kind, wise, courageous, and a splendid manager, was helped by the capable step-daughter Mary in feeding, clothing, and educating this large and mixed family. The father was in the Postal Service, and the summers were spent in Naini Tal where Jim and Archie went to school, and the winters in the foothills below in their house at Kaladhungi. In both places there was much to do. Naini, with its fine lake, provided boating and fishing and many other sports; but Kaladhungi was the Corbett and Doyle playground and holiday home. It was there that Tom, Jim's eldest brother and his hero, taught the small boy how to handle a gun. When he was still quite a little boy, Jim would go off into the jungle to camp. At night, as he has described, he would light a fire, and when a tiger or leopard and other wild animals came too near, he would throw another log on, make the fire blaze, and the animals would move off. It was on these expeditions that he learnt his early lessons in jungle lore, and acquired that passion for the jungle, its flora and wildlife that made him feel that time out of it was time lost. It was his familiarity with it that made him the undisputed master of it. Blessed with abnormally good eyesight, keen hearing, remarkable memory, and powers of observation, coupled with a toughness that was almost miraculous and great courage, he had all the equipment to make him the Sherlock Holmes of the forest. He sang well and, being a good mimic, he could imitate the calls of the animals. Often you will read of how he imitated a bird or a barking deer, and often a tiger seeking a mate. The Thak man-eater owes his death to being deceived by Jim's calling.

School days over, Jim was anxious to get a job quickly, for the family finances were always a worry. An important man in the Province granted him an interview, but when he saw him, he said he was too young. Jim replied 'You tell me I am too young to begin to work, but if I came next year you would tell me I was too old'. Later, he accepted the temporary post of Fuel Inspector on the railway. He enjoyed this, and was able to travel about on the engines, and even drive them. So well did he do the job that he was offered the post of Transhipment Inspector with the Bengal and North-Western Railway (BNWR) at Mokameh Ghat. He was then only twenty. In *My India*, the last five chapters of the book are concerned with Mokameh Ghat, and exciting and moving they are. Some space should be given to this for it was an important crisis in his life. On pay of under £10 a month and with no other capital, he was asked to take over the contract for handling and trans-shipping goods. This work had been done in part by a labour company, but they had melted away for their homes and the harvest. There was no labour, and Jim had to recruit it. He quickly made a friend of the station master. Together, they sought out ten headmen and each was asked to recruit ten labourers. That was a start only, for the job was stupendous. Mokameh Ghat was the junction of a railway of narrow gauge connecting with a ferry system which took goods across the Ganges to a broad-gauge railway. Four hundred wagons were waiting to be unloaded, and a thousand on the other side of the river, all fully loaded, were waiting to be ferried across. Moreover, there were some 400 broad-gauge wagons to be unloaded. It was estimated that 15,000 tons of goods had to be shifted and got on their way. And, daily, fresh wagons were arriving. Jim was undaunted despite the terms of his contract: 1 shilling and 8 pence for every 35 tons shifted. It was the lowest rate paid to any contractor in India. He and his men worked from 4 a.m. to 8 p.m. daily, including Sundays, with no stop. The accumulated mass of wagons began to disappear, but the railway authorities failed to send the cash. For weeks the men were not paid, and they had insufficient food, but they never gave in. No answer having been received to his letters, Jim sent an ultimatum. He telegraphed that all work would cease at noon next day unless the cash was forthcoming. That did the trick. For twenty-one years Jim worked at Mokameh Ghat, and the traffic never accumulated but always flowed smoothly.

Jim wanted to go to the war in South Africa, but the railways would not release him. When the 1914 war broke out, he went at once to Calcutta to apply for a Commission. He was thirty-nine then, and was too old. By 1917, the regulations had become easier, and he helped to raise a labour force of 5000, recruiting his men in Kumaon. Of these, he took 500 to France. There, he was a father to every one of his men and, at the end of the war he brought back 499 and re-settled them in their villages. He was then a Major, and was soon sent to Afghanistan where he saw fighting. On his return to civil life, with characteristic generosity, he gave the whole of his war bonus to a fund for building a canteen for the troops.

Jim Corbett's errands of mercy in hunting and destroying man-eaters covered thirty-two years, 1907–39. He so far excelled any other hunter that immense pressure was put on him to drop his work and leave for the afflicted district, sometimes for several weeks on end, to rid it of the trouble. Often, the ordeals were terrible: two or three days with no food, squatting motionless for hours in a tree, cramped and soaked through with sweat or rain. In all, he shot twelve man-eating tigers and leopards, and these had accounted for at least 1500 deaths among the villagers of Kumaon. There is no guessing how many more would have died but for Jim.

Jim loved the forests and their inhabitants—with the exception of snakes, he had no enemies. For the tiger he had great respect, and he held him in awe, and was unhappy at the prospect of its ultimate extermination. When a tiger turned man-eater, he believed and proved that this was due to a wound or some accident that prevented the beast from killing its normal prey. Sometimes, porcupine quills were found in its mouth and these had set up inflammation. 'A tiger is a large-hearted gentleman with boundless courage', he wrote; and no better epitaph could be found for Jim himself. He put himself on equal terms with these beasts, studied them and understood them, knew their tactics, and knew how to out-manoeuvre them. To shoot a man-eater very naturally gave him great 'satisfaction at having done a job that badly needed doing'. The satisfaction also came from having out-manoeuvred, on his own ground, a very worthy antagonist. And, 'the greatest satisfaction of all came from having made a small portion of the earth safe for a brave little girl to walk on'. So he writes at the end of the story of *The Muktesar Man-Eater*. Perhaps the finest year of his life was 1910. In that year, he records that he shot the Muktesar tiger and the Panar leopard (this one had a toll of 400 villagers) and, in between and with no mechanical help, had set up an all-time record at Mokameh Ghat by handling 5,500 tons of goods in a single day.

Jim did sometimes shoot for sport, and Viceroys and Governors would stay with him, or have their camp set up near his home, and he would organize the shoots. But, as the years passed, he enjoyed this sport less and less and, by good fortune, the late Lord Strathcona gave him a 16-mm Cine Kodak. This was a new joy to him and, for the future it was to be stalking with a camera and not with a rifle.

Here again, his fearlessness and infinite patience produced wildlife pictures that have never been equalled. Nobody else has called up six tigers, the nearest 8 feet and the farthest 30 feet away, and produced a hundred or more feet of film. For three months, he would go before dawn to a pool and make his tiger calls and, at last, he got this magnificent group together. The nearest tiger is looking straight at the camera, and he yawns. Some are crouching on a rock at the back while two others are restlessly pacing up and down. Answering questions about this film, he said he had not taken a rifle with him. But he did have an old Kapok cushion which he had decided to throw at any tiger which came for him! To cover the sound of the clockwork in the camera, he had kept up a succession of jungle bird and animal noises. This film, and others of wildlife in India and Africa, is in the Natural History Museum, London.

Jim was sixty-four when the Second World War broke out and, clearly, he was now too old to fight; but from 1940–2, he served as Vice-President of the District Soldier's Board, and recruited 1400 men from Kumaon for a Pioneer Corps. Then, he became desperately ill with typhus, and it looked as though he would have to be an invalid for the rest of his life. But he made a slow but complete recovery and, in 1944, he was commissioned Lieutenant Colonel, and put in charge of training men for warfare in the jungles of Burma. Here, he was in his element, and no more perfect teacher for the job could have been found. Again, he was struck down, and this time with a serious bout of malaria, and for a long time he was laid up. His services to India were rewarded with the Kaisar-I-Hind Gold medal, the CSI and the OBE. The Government of India granted him the Freedom of the Forests, a privilege only given once previously. In 1957, after his death, the Government decreed that a game sanctuary, established largely by his efforts in Garhwal in 1935, should henceforth be known as 'The Corbett National Park' 'in memory of one who had dedicated his life to the service of the simple hill-folk of Kumaon'. His life had, indeed, been dedicated to these people, and the reader will learn for himself how often he came near to death for their sakes. It would have been difficult to find one of his people that would not have cheerfully given his life for 'Corbett Sahib'. And this could also be true of his mother in her lifetime, and his sisters who had in the house, a little surgery where those with sores, wounds, snakebites, and fever would all go for free treatment.

He was in his seventieth year when he sent to the Oxford University Press in Bombay the typescript of what was to become *The Man-Eaters of Kumaon*. This was based largely on a small, privately printed book called *Jungle Stories*. He had expected little, and was delighted when he was told that this was magnificent stuff and that great things would come of it. And so they did. Hundreds of thousands of copies have been sold in all parts of the world, and have been read eagerly by 'Dons' and school boys, and translations have been published in eighteen languages. His royalties he gave, in large part, to the blind in England and India. Though critics have likened him to Kipling, beyond the fact that both wrote of India, Kipling's stories, for the most part, are fiction while Jim's are true in every detail. Kipling was a far more professional writer, while Jim tells his adventures simply, and in a way that seems exactly right for his subject matter. There is never a false or jarring note. Everything is set down as he experienced it and saw it. So keenly were his experiences felt by him that he said he could live through each, and retrace his steps to the final kill with no difficulty. Here is the marriage of memory and observation. That this was true can be shown by reading the letters he wrote to his sister when out after a man-eater. Whenever he could, he would send her a letter describing his adventurous day. He never re-read these letters. Yet, writing thirty or forty years later, his letters and his book agree perfectly in every detail. He kept no diaries...

'The Nightjar's Egg' and the story 'Robin' prove his love of birds and dogs. On his bird table at home would come specimens of almost every bird in the district, and many he would tame so that they would sit on his hand or shoulder. His friends were many, and extended from Viceroys and Governors to the humblest 'untouchable'. One of his books he dedicates to the 'poor people of India, among whom I have lived and whom I love'. In the foothills there was a village called Choti Haldwani. It was almost derelict, and only a handful of peasants were living there. Jim bought it, and threw himself into the work of making it a model village. He fenced it against marauding wild animals, opened up a water supply, cleared the jungle, and cut out of the village forty holdings. Then he built new houses, and repaired the best of the old. He planted fruit trees, and gave the people vegetable seeds for their plots, paid all the taxes, and kept this up after he left India.

In 1947 came the Partition, and Jim and his sister, not only for that reason but for others too, decided that their best course was to leave for Kenya. Jim had frequently visited that country, and he was a joint owner of a coffee estate. It was a terrible wrench for them and a sad day for the people of Kumaon. Old friends and villagers made the long journey to Bombay to see them off, bringing with them their presents and tears.

The Corbetts finally settled in Nyeri, and found a happy home in the bungalow built by Lord Baden-Powell. In the forests, Jim was able to pursue his photography of wildlife, and he was made an honorary Game Warden...

In 1955, *Tree Tops*, his last book was published. It is an account of the visit of the royal couple* to the little hotel named Tree Tops built

* Tree Tops Hotel is a hotel in Aberdare National Park in Kenya near the township of Nyeri, 1,966 m (6,450 ft) above sea level on the Aberdare Range

in a large tree above a pool and a resort of big game. They spent an afternoon and a night there and in the early morning the news was brought that King George VI had died.

On 19 April 1955, Jim suffered a severe heart attack and died in hospital. He lies in the cemetery at Nyeri where that other master of tracking, Baden-Powell, is also buried.

Jim was tall and spare, and kept to the end of his life the figure of a young man. No-one failed to notice the blueness of his eyes, his shy and compassionate expression which easily and frequently changed to a warm smile. Simple, modest, quiet in manner, and a delightful talker, he was a man to whom everyone was attracted. Many have felt his saintly quality, and none can deny that he was a great man.

———————

and in sight of Mount Kenya. First opened in 1932, it was literally built into the tops of the trees of Aberdare National Park as a tree house, offering the guests a close view of the local wildlife in complete safety. The idea was to provide a machan (hunting platform on a tree during shikar in India) experience in relative safety and comfort. From the original modest two-room tree house, it has grown into fifty rooms.

Treetops shot into media limelight when Princess Elizabeth, along with her husband Prince Philip, learned of the death of her father, George VI, which occurred on 6 February 1952, the night she was at Treetops, while in Kenya. She returned immediately to Britain. Corbett, a resident of Treetops at the time, wrote the now famous lines in the visitors' log book: 'For the first time in the history of the world, a young girl climbed into a tree one day a Princess and after having what she described as her most thrilling experience she climbed down from the tree next day a Queen—God bless her.'

The Universal Appeal of Jim Corbett
Letters and Reviews

Man-Eaters of Kumaon

The Man-Eaters of Kumaon is Jim Corbett's own story of his experiences in the Kumaon hills, which lie in the Himalayas in the far northern United Provinces of India, where man-eating tigers have long been the scourge and terror of the tiny villages and jungles. To the excitement of the chase and the kill, which Major Corbett imparts in a simple and direct but vivid and dramatic style, is added a picture of jungle life that is rare in the history of literature of this kind. His love of nature, his knowledge of jungle ways, his keen observation of wildlife, have all played their part in creating a story of the cunning and cruelty of the man-eater pitted against the courage and resourcefulness of man.

—Marinette, *Wisconsin Eagle-Star,*
12 April 1945.

Introducing Major Corbett's book, Lord Linlithgow, who was Viceroy of India 1936–43, writes: 'Having spent in Major Corbett's company some part of such holidays as I have contrived to take during my time in India, I can with confidence write of him that no man with whom I have hunted in any continent better understands the signs of the jungle.'

No one can read far in this book without realizing how true these words are. One also discovers very soon that Major Corbett is not merely a big-game hunter killing for the love of it. The tigers he shot were all dangerous man-eaters and had to be killed. Only once did Major Corbett have any regrets, and that was when he shot a sleeping tiger, although his action was entirely justified. Sportsmen, however, will appreciate his attitude.

What Tigers are Not

Before describing his exploits, Major Corbett gives some interesting information about tigers. 'Human beings are not the natural prey of tigers, and it is only when tigers have been incapacitated through wounds or old age that, in order to live, they are compelled to take to a diet of human flesh.'

A diet of human flesh evidently agrees with tigers, as all man-eaters, in the author's experience, had remarkably fine coats. Again, the popular belief that the cubs of man-eaters automatically become the same is not borne out by facts. Then, sometimes there is a doubt as to whether or not the killer has been a tiger or a leopard. As a general rule—and Major Corbett has seen no exceptions to this—man-eaters always kill by day, and leopards in the dark.

Major Corbett also disagrees with the descriptions 'as cruel as a tiger' and 'as bloodthirsty as a tiger'. The tiger, in general, is neither of these things. He writes: 'I have not seen a case where a tiger has been deliberately cruel or where it has been bloodthirsty to the extent that it has killed, without provocation, more than it has needed to satisfy its hunger or the hunger of its cubs.'

His considered opinion is that the tiger is a large-hearted gentleman with boundless courage, and that when he is exterminated—as exterminated he will be unless public opinion rallies to his support—India will be the poorer by having lost the finest of her fauna.

Pushed off by Feet

The incidents in this book are tremendously exciting, the more so as they are told without frills. There is the almost incredible story of the Indian, pinned down by a tiger which had already savaged him, putting his feet under its belly, and pushing it off so that it fell down a perpendicular hillside.

There is the man-eater on which Major Corbett came upon suddenly while he was carrying some eggs in his left hand. On this occasion the beast was a tigress. She was lying with her forepaws stretched out and her hind legs well tucked under her, 'and on her face was a smile similar to that one sees on the face of a dog welcoming his master home after a long absence'.

Here was a predicament: the tigress, still smiling, kept her eyes fixed on Major Corbett, who had to sling around his rifle to shoot. This he did by an almost imperceptible movement, three-quarters of a circle, and he shot the tigress. He realized later that the eggs, which remained unbroken, had been helpful, for had both hands been free he would have swung round quickly, and his movements might have made the tigress spring.

Nearly Died of Fright

There is an exciting description of another tiger shot by Major Corbett, and not killed until later. It went mad, and for half an hour, roaring horribly, attacked a fallen tree and tore it to bits. During that scene, Major Corbett says, 'I nearly died of fright.' And here is another vivid and terrible scene: 'A rock cliff with a narrow ledge running partly across it and ending in a little depression in which an injured woman is lying; a young girl frozen with terror on the ledge, and a tiger slowly creeping towards her; retreat in every direction cut off, and no help at hand.'

Throughout, this book is packed with incident. Some of the stories are breathtaking; all are worth telling. There has been nothing like it since Lieutenant-Colonel Patterson's *The Man-Eaters of Tsavo*, a book beside which it is in every way worthy to take its place.

—*The Glasgow Herald*, 19 September 1946

Oxford University Press celebrated the publication of Jim Corbett's *Man-Eaters of Kumaon* on April 4 with a cocktail party in the ballroom of the Hotel Pierre for the New York book trade and two visiting tiger cubs. The tigers, twelve weeks old and very sleepy, were flown to New York from Florida in a private plane by their owner, Captain Roman Proske, Director of the North Miami Zoological Gardens. The cubs stamped their footprints on a copy of the book which will be sent to the author at his home in India. Colonel Corbett was unable to get reservations to New York to celebrate the publication of his book.

Man-Eaters of Kumaon, which was originally scheduled for publication last fall, was postponed when it was chosen as a Book-of-the-Month Club selection for April.

There are now 489,000 copies in print, including the Book-of-the-Month Club edition. The book will have a major campaign throughout the country, and the first ads, featuring a huge tiger footprint, have already appeared in full pages in the *New York Herald Tribune Weekly* Book Review, the *New York Times* Book Review and the *Chicago Sun's* Book Week.

With the publication of *Man-Eaters of Kumaon*, Oxford is making the first commercial use of the 'black light' paper used in charts and maps in combat planes during the war. A limited number of book jackets and bookstore posters have been treated with luminescent inks which make them glow in the dark. Oxford bought up a small amount of luminescent paper which Crocker Burbank, the largest manufactures of the paper during the war, had left over, enough for 600 jackets. The titles and the eyes and teeth of the tiger shown on the jacket have been printed by silk screen with fluorescent ink which will glow when subjected to a black light, in bookstores with window light fixtures which will take a black lamp. The lamps have been provided, after considerable effort, by Oxford. Posters designed by Mike Gross, featuring a picture by the animal artist, Jules Gotlieb, have also been treated with fluorescent ink. The Doubleday shops in New York inaugurated these displays on April 5 and later, the books, posters and black lights will be sent to other shops.

—*Publisher's Weekly*, New York, 13 April 1946.

Also out of a hobby grew one of the most exciting books of hunting stories published in many a day, this too a Book-of-the-Month Club selection, Jim Corbett's *Man-Eaters of Kumaon*. Even in retrospect, the experiences of this Indian-born Englishman, as he tracked down the various great cats, will bring back a thrill of terror. Before his book was brought to a close, Mr Corbett stated that he planned to give up hunting of these tigers which deserved death for the reason that they had killed hundreds of human beings. He thought it but fair to his family—one sister with whom he lived—and perhaps to himself, after years of strain, to spend his life more quietly.

But now it seems that the 74-year-old stalker of wild beasts has gone out after another man-eater. Every admirer of Jim Corbett will wish him well, and pray for a safe return to the writing of his second book, *The Man-Eating Leopard of Rudraprayag*.

When Mr Corbett's first book was launched, his publishers gave a cocktail party in the Cotillion Room of the Hotel Pierre, New York. Mr Corbett could not be there, but a great many of the literati were and, as the Book-of-the-Month Club News tells the story, the honoured guests were two tiger cubs, aged three months, the offspring of the largest tiger in the United States, flown up from Miami for the occasion.

The cubs were in a small cage and evidently didn't mind that. The guests preferred it. The latter admired the cubs for their bold stripes, solid white triangle markings on their ears, were calling them the handsomest things they had ever seen. But the size of their paws amazed them. These the cubs used as they pummelled one another, growled, bared their strong white teeth. And readers of Mr Corbett remembered that it is with these teeth that the tiger kills, and not with a stroke of the heavy paws.

—*Watertown NY Daily Times*, 11 June 1946.

My dear Corbett,

… You may remember you authorized us to produce an abridged edition of the *Man-Eaters of Kumaon* [titled *The Mohan Man-Eater and Other Stories*] for schools. This is now nearing publication and I hope to send you a copy next month. C.H.G. Moorhouse has done some quite good illustrations and there are a few notes and exercises but the stories themselves are essentially yours and I do not think you will find anything objectionable. We are, of course, hoping to have very large sales of this edition in India…

—Roy E. Hawkins' letter to Jim Corbett,

31 August 1948

The Mohan Man-Eater and Other Stories

Always thrilling, hunting becomes a dangerous gamble with the hunter's own life at stake as well, when the quarry is a dreaded man-eater. And still more interesting and exciting is the tale when told by Jim Corbett, whose modest and straightforward account of his encounters with a number of man-eating tigers makes the story an unassuming, but nevertheless fascinating, classic tale of big-game hunting.

Abridged and slightly simplified, these stories from Jim Corbett's justly famous, *Man-Eaters of Kumaon* provide excellent reading for school students, and are the best possible introduction to the original volume as well as to several other remarkable records of this vigorous pastime. Questions and notes at the end render them more useful while illustrations by Moorhouse make them more attractive. Elementary information about a 12-bore shot gun, a double-barrel riffle, and the working mechanism of a magazine rifle on the front endpaper will prove helpful to the students.

The author's still more existing tale, *The Man-Eating Leopard of Rudraprayag* should also be abridged and made available to the students.

—*The Progress of Education*, Sept.–Dec. 1948.

These stories are taken from the author's *Man-Eaters of Kumaon*, and have been abridged and simplified for school reading. The black and white illustrations are by C.H.G. Moorhouse.

Boys and even girls of the middle school stage like reading of this kind—packed as it is with the thrill of adventure, danger, and courage. The book is suitable for the library or as an extra reader.

—*The Ceylon Teacher*, March 1949

Those who have read Jim Corbett's books, *The Man-Eaters of Kumaon* and *The Man-Eating Leopard of Rudraprayag*, will rejoice to see that selections from the former of these are now available in an edition, abridged and slightly simplified for school reading. The book is well-printed and beautifully illustrated. It could be given as a present to any child with a normal love of adventure—one hesitates to recommend it also to grown-ups only because, while they will not need the final seven pages of questions and notes, they will value the editorial matter in the original edition. A really first-class book for children.

—*U.S.C.L. Bookman*, Madras, January 1949

The book under review is a collection of stories from Jim Corbett's world famous book *Man-Eaters of Kumaon*. Lord Linlithgow, the ex-Viceroy of India, in the course of a foreword on *Man-Eaters of Kumaon*, says that the stories contained therein were true accounts of the author's experience with man-eating tigers in the jungles of the United Provinces. 'Jim Corbett's name is already a house-hold word in Kumaon,' says M.G. Hallet, ex-Governor of United Provinces. But by now every literate man knows him. Jim Corbett's narration of his experiences in the form of stories is very descrip-tive and lucid. The book under review derives its name from one of the stories of the original book, and contains, along with it other stories, viz., 'Champawat Man-Eater' and 'Chowgarh Man-Eater'. These stories are suitably abridged and simplified as they are meant for use in schools.

The sponsors who have advocated the inclusion of this book in the curriculum of schools are to be congratulated. The study of such stories is sure to inculcate in a boy the courage, patience, presence of mind, and persistence which were responsible for Jim Corbett's successful career as a hunter of man-eaters.

—*Madras Information*, 15 March 1949

The Man-Eating Leopard of Rudraprayag

At Rudraprayag, two rivers—the Mandakini coming down from Kedarnath, and the Alakananda from Badrinath—meet, and the present story is about the unholy depredations of a man-eating leopard at the supremely holy place of Rudraprayag. To a person living in Assam and Bengal, a man-eater would seem to be a Royal Bengal tiger (*Dhekiya-patiya*) and not the smaller leopard (*Nahar-phutuki*) who is, by the way, more cunning and mischievous than his more dignified fellow creature. The particular leopard whose activities Colonel Corbett so absorbingly narrates was credited with more than 120 human victims. It is impossible in a review to give an idea of the uncanny swiftness and stealth with which the leopard bagged his victims, and it is equally difficult to suggest the thrill one will have when going through the hazards which Colonel Corbett faced in tracking down the leopard. An old classic of this type was the *Man-Eaters of Tsavo* by Patterson; the present work will possibly be another such classic with a lasting interest.

—*The Assam Herald*, 21 November 1948.

Terror gripped large areas in the Garhwal district for several years. With the approach of dusk, 'curfew' was enforced on the area much more strictly than at any time under British rule; some people even attributed all their trouble to ghosts. But the real mischief-maker was a man-eating leopard, which had acquired such cunning as to defeat the most brainy attempts to kill it. It could avoid traps; it would reject portions of its 'kill' which had been poisoned; it would avoid moonlit patches of ground when a 'shikari' was covering it from a 'machan' in some nearby tree; one day, it even coolly took its place inside a room in a house before its inhabitants came in and snatched off the boy at the tail end of the group. Anyone who ventured outside his house at night was as good as lost. The leopard was even bold enough, at times, to tear down doors and snatch its victim from inside. The Government of U.P.* was forced to move in the matter, as the press of the whole country was raising a protest against the depredations of the man-eater. Mr Jim Corbett, with experience of big game-hunting in Africa and India, at last came on the scene and, after several attempts, which were failures in spite of his drawing on all his past experiences and capacity to plan, he killed it—with a shot in the dark. The leopard was to the last master-hand at fooling its hunters—which it did, even in death. An interesting narrative, with plenty of unusual information about the denizens of the forest.

—*Bombay Chronicle Weekly*, 21 November 1948.

Jungle Lore

The now famous author of *Man-Eaters of Kumaon* presents his fourth effort, in which he sets out to present 'all I have learnt in a lifetime of Jungle Lore'. In part autobiographical, we get glimpses into the childhood and early years of the author; with him we go through our first lessons in safety precautions; go out shooting for the first time; and share the thrill and delight when he is presented with his first gun and rifle.

The author narrates a number of stories and incidents from his vast experience, and we are shown step by step how a truly great shikari is made. In spite of the author's avowed purpose to present what he has learnt of jungle lore, let not the reader think that all he will need to bring his first tiger to bag is to acquire a rifle and a copy of this book; it is not intended as a textbook on Tiger Hunting.

* The United Provinces.

Some of the descriptions of our glorious jungles and the wildlife therein will bring to old-timers nostalgic memories of the good old days. One hopes that the not-so-old-timers will realize what they are missing by the continued indiscriminate destruction of game, and appreciate the urgent need for the protection and preservation of our fauna and flora.

Although the book makes extremely interesting reading, it does not quite live up to the reputation of the author's earlier efforts, nor did it meet your reviewer's expectations.

—M.R.S.C., *The Journal of the Bombay Natural History Society*,
August–December 1954

Jim Corbett's new book is chiefly about his own education in the art and craft of being in the jungle without feeling afraid and actually loving it; fear in this case being from something unknown or unexplained. The only way out of this, according to him, is a thorough knowledge of the forest, and an acquired taste for it. In the last chapter, he describes Jungle Sensitiveness, and the development of a subconscious warning of danger.

Corbett has genuine respect for the material he worked in with intimate acquaintance; but he refrains from seeing human traits in animals or 'philosophizing' in some such direction. An occasional aside does not jar when it comes from his pen, as a direct conclusion from experience.

'My happiness, I believe, resulted from the fact that all wildlife is happy in its natural surroundings. In nature, there is no sorrow and no repining. The jungle folk, *in their natural surroundings*, do not kill but for want only. When I was ignorant, I tried to rescue birds and young animals caught by hawks or by eagles, and deer caught by carnivorous beasts, but soon found that in trying to rescue one, I caused the death of two.'

—*The Times of India*, 5 August 1954

National Servicemen, not long out of Malaya or Kenya, may have some difficulty in sharing Jim Corbett's enthusiasm. He visited the jungles he writes about for the purpose of shikar, and he describes his 'unalloyed happiness' in life which revealed another world. Yet, in spite of their grim tasks, many of our boys also fell in love with the jungles in which they found themselves campaigning, and for that reason they will enjoy and understand this fascinating book.

—*Services and Territorial Magazine*, London

Those who have read Col Corbett's *Man-Eaters of Kumaon* and *The Man-Eating Leopard of Rudraprayag* will not find in his latest book the tense, absorbing narrative with which he described his awe-inspiring searches for, and successful encounters with, tiger and leopard. But this is a book which is equally fascinating in its own right.

Corbett gives us the benefit of his many years of unparalleled experiences in Indian jungles, and reveals his deep affection for the wildlife of which he has seen so much. He starts from his boyhood, and there is a good deal of autobiographical detail which makes his readers know this intrepid man a little better.

A grand book for the winter fireside, for those who like their thrills in comfort. No one can say this of Col Corbett.

—*Shields Gazette*,
26 November 1953

My India

The Last of the Sahibs

Jim Corbett is one of the last Englishmen to write on India in the tradition of the Sahibs. Those who have read his *Man-Eaters of Kumaon* will remember how excitingly he describes animals. In his new book, *My India* (Oxford University Press, 10s. 6d.), he writes just as vividly and interestingly about human beings.

'Tilni was a clean-limbed attractive young girl, some eighteen years of age. Her hair, done in a foot-high cone in the traditional manner of the women of Terai, was draped in a white-bordered black sari, her upper person was encased in a tight-fitting red bodice, and a voluminous gaily coloured skirt completed her costume. When asked by Anderson why she had left her husband, she pointed to Chadi and said, "Look at him. Not only is he dirty, as you can see, but he is also a miser ..."'

Most of Corbett's characters are hill tribesmen on the borders of Tibet and Nepal. They are no more representative Indian that Finnish Laplanders are typical Europeans. They have one thing in common with the Indian people as a whole, and that is their poverty. It is a pity, therefore, that Corbett has gone out of his way to impress us that he is writing of 'the real Indian—the Indian whose loyalty and devotion alone made it possible for a handful of men to administer, for close on two hundred years, a vast subcontinent, with its teeming millions'.

This kind of propaganda frequently hits the pot with a hollow sound. The old Imperialism, whatever its merits or demerits, is dead in India; it serves no more useful purpose to resurrect it in this book than King Charles' head in Dick's Memorial. Unfortunately, Corbett also emulates Mr Dick's mistake in that he is constantly trying to put some of his trouble out of King Charles' head into ours.

All the old Sahib's assumptions are brought back again: that Indian loyalty means loyalty to British rulers, that Indian courage means dying as a soldier under the Sahib's command. It is not strange that Corbett did not hear the words Quisling and Mercenary in the hills; but it is tragic that he appears never to have thought that patriotic Indians might see their collaborating countrymen in those terms.

Even now, from the heights of Kenya where he has found a home since Indian Independence, he cannot see. A man of integrity, a good hunter and brave, he is still blind to the feelings and aspirations of the people among whom he lived for twenty-one years. That is the complete and tragic picture of the Sahib in India. But that complete story is told in *My India* only for those who can read between the lines.

All this has (thank heavens!) its amusing side. Such sweeping generalizations as 'Indians do not get hay fever' would bring a reproachful look to the eyes of more than one Bengali friend of mine whom I have seen sneezing and swollen-nosed in the struggle with this torturing complaint. The statement 'I never inquired into the private affairs of my work people, for Indians are sensitive on that point' staggers me. That a man, as warm-hearted and generous as Corbett reveals himself to be, has not discovered that such inquiries are the common custom of the Indian people, extended even to strangers in a railway carriage, is amazing and revealing.

I once met two Scots planters who claimed to love 'the coolies' on their tea estate in Assam 'like brothers'. They were perfectly sincere in believing that this was the case. But when they heard that in India I lived in the same house with the 'natives', wore their dress, ate their food, and felt for them exactly as I did for my English friends, they were horrified.

'But laddie,' the more brotherly of the two cried aghast, 'you can no' do that any more! Come to Assam an' we'll give you a bed with us.'

In vain I assured the hospitable pair that I stayed with Indians through choice, that I thoroughly enjoyed it, and that my host at the moment was also my best friend—not a 'coolie' but a Doctor of Philosophy of London University, my words meant nothing to them. All they could say was: 'But this is India, laddie. You canna do it here.'

They were both kindly men, and were deeply hurt when I suggested that their fondness for Indians was similar to the fondness they accorded to a dearly beloved dog.

Although lacking in imagination to put himself in the other man's place, Corbett has written an absorbing and moving account of his relations with poor hill tribesmen among whom he earned his living as a Railway Fuel Inspector for many years. While there is some evidence that he loved them as he loved the jungle animals, tigers in particular, there is also evidence that he could sympathize with and heal their material wounds. The tribute he pays to Chamari, whom he does not fail to stress 'belongs to the lowest strata of India's sixty million Untouchables', is a sincere and beautiful one. Chamari had nursed a railway worker who had cholera, and when he in his turn, fell a victim to the disease, Corbett nursed him.

'Hushed people who had watched with me during those long hours were either sitting on the ground or standing around when Chamari suddenly sat up and in an urgent and perfectly natural voice said, "Maharaj, Maharaj! Where are you?" I was standing at the head of the bed, and when I leant forward and put my hand on his shoulder, he caught it in both his and said, "Maharaj, Parmeshwar (correctly Parmesvara, the Universal Spirit) is calling me and I must go." Then, putting his hands together and bowing his head, he said, "Parmeshwar, I come." He was dead when I laid him back on the bed.'

The story ends in a way that would greatly touched Mahatma Gandhi, who had a very warm place in his heart for the 'Untouchables', whom he called Harijans, the children of God. A Brahmin (priest of the highest caste) slips off his sandals and makes obeisance at the feet of the dead Chamari. He says: 'I have found what I have been searching for ... My master the head priest, hearing of the good deeds of this man, sent me to find him and take him to the temple, that he may have *darshan* of him.'

It is a noble tale, a Brahmin asking for a Harijan's blessing, and one of the best in the book. One wishes that the only reference to Mahatma Gandhi that Corbett makes was not to link him with the repute of Miss Kathleen Mayo.

There are several vignettes in a lighter key: 'Lalajee', a story that bears out Corbett's thesis that 'the poor in India never forget a kindness'; 'Budhu', the rescue of a coal shoveller from the clutches of a nasty type of moneylender. But it is in the dramatic moment—often the death-dealing moment—that the author excels.

The Havildar was sitting on the ground with his back to a tree, his shirt was open, and on the nipple of his left breast there was a spot of blood. Freddy produced a flask and put it to the Havildar's lips, but the man shook his head and put the flask aside, saying, 'It is wine. I cannot drink it.' When pressed he added, 'All my life I have been an abstainer, and I cannot got to my Creator with wine on my lips. I am thirsty and crave a little water.'

Corbett really understands his humans. In such passages, he can identify himself with a man trapped in superstition, dying for an idea which others before him have believed in. He is less convincing when he indulges in pipe-dreams about how wonderful things were in India when Sahibs were Sahibs.

I am thankful that my men and I served in India at a time when the interest of one was the interest of all, and when Hindu, Mohammedan, depressed class, and Christian could live, work, and play together in perfect harmony.

Was it ever so delightful and simple as that?

I will not quote the passages in which Corbett is at his worst, where he takes up Kathleen Mayo's[†] muck-rake and turns over the old rubbish: child-marriage, dacoits, and the like. We do not regard the British way of life as being fairly represented by the crime ration that appears in the sensational press. Why not be equally fair to India?

By all means read this book. It makes exciting reading. But while reading, beware not only of the tigers, but of the last Sahibs who make bitter enemies for us in Asia where we can least afford to have them.

—Dennis Gray Stoll, *John O'London's Weekly*,
Vol. LXI, No. 1449, 18 April 1952

Sir,

I feel that I must write to protest against the grossly unfair review of Jim Corbett's *My India* published in *John O' London's Weekly* of April 18th. The whole review contains so many half-truths and misrepresentations that it must inevitably prejudice many readers against buying an extremely fine book.

Dennis Gray Stoll says that most of the book is devoted to hill tribesmen, whereas a good third is about life at Mokameh Ghat, in

---

[†] Katherine Mayo (27 January 1867–9 October 1940) was an American writer notorious for her polemical book *Mother India* (1927), in which she attacked the Hindu society, religion, and culture of the country. The book created a sensation since its main theme was against the demands for self-rule and Indian Independence. Mayo wrote negatively about the treatment of India's women, the *Untouchables*, the animals, the dirt, and the character of its nationalistic politicians.

Bengal, where Corbett spent over twenty years as a trans-shipment inspector.

He spent only eighteen months as a Railway Fuel Inspector, as your reviewer would have discovered if he had read the book properly. Where in the book does Mr Stoll find passages to support his indictment of Corbett that 'Indian courage means dying as a soldier under a Sahib's command'? All the examples cited by Corbett are of courage displayed in the face of adversity, disease, and the attacks of wild animals.

The statement that Corbett takes up Kathleen Mayo's muck-rake to turn over the old rubbish about child-marriage and dacoits is pure nonsense. Corbett's references to child-marriage and dacoity are purely incidental to the stories he tells and he passes no words of censure on either. In fact, he professes a certain liking and much tolerant sympathy for the notorious dacoit Sultana.

Mr Stoll is obviously well-satisfied with himself for having lived in the same house as Indians, wearing their clothes, and eating their food. Would he have given his life's savings to an Indian for the latter to restart his business after nursing him through an attack of the dreaded disease cholera, as Corbett did?

Where there is anything in the book to make bitter enemies for us in Asia it is beyond my power to find.

—Letter to the Editor, *John O' London's Weekly*,
16 May 1952 (by Harold Hal, Meadow Drive,
Ashbourne Road, Belper, Derby)

As Jim Corbett has made it amply clear in the introductory remark, this is not a history of India, or an account of the rise and fall of the British Raj, nor yet of the cleaving of the subcontinent particularly, and Asia in general. He lived, he says, too near the seat of events and too intimately associated with the actors to get the right perspective for recording such momentous matters and events.

So far so good. We are grateful to the author for sparing our feelings and sentiments and loading us with another 'biased' history as so many Europeans have tried to burden us with. Jim is frank if anything, and as transparent as a glass of pane, and his truth and honesty are as proverbial as anyone in Mokameh Ghat, where he worked for the major part of his life, will testify and vouch for. One feels, however, that if corbett HAD decided to write a history, we would have been proud of his effort, for it would have been factual, true, and not coloured by nationality, religious, or social bias and beliefs.

What then could a European's pretensions be to call another country his own, and refuse to subscribe to Kipling's belief that the 'East is East and West is West and never the twain could meet!' Many foreigners have declared their love for our country, and have given tangible manifestation of the same by settling down here and even adopting our customs and religions and affecting our manners, names, and clothes. But Jim retained his individuality, his religion, and clothes, and yet he was literally loved by many and given an affection that was denied their own. A perusal of the book will make it amply clear why.

Four hundred million people whose only prayer to god and the government in being is to give them security of life and their daily bread; an honest, simple, brave, loyal, hard-working people often described as India's starving millions, among whom he lived and whom he loved—it is of these of whom he writes, with a fervour and enthusiasm that can only stem from deep love of the subject he writes about. His sketch of village life is artistic and picturesque in its very simplicity, and accounts of his work as a railway contractor at

Mokameh Ghat at Patna, are monuments to a man's ingenuity and brave fight against overwhelming odds, sustained by the love of his fellow workers bore him. Most of the scenes centre round Naini Tal, his home, which he bequeathed to the U.P. Government and the hill people, his special love.

A lover of India and Indians, he gave all he had to the poor of India and, in fact, jeopardized his health and risked his life many times to help rid a hill village of a man-eater, so that the roads may be safer for them to walk on. It is in the capacity of a hunter that Jim Corbett achieved fame and it is as such that we know him and love him most. He eschewed politics and hated it like the very devil or plague.

His many admirable traits and the hidden side of his character, his charitable disposition and readiness to lend a helping hand whenever and wherever needed, we learn from the hill people who render a glowing account of the Sahib, punctuated by many a tear. The UP Government has done well to perpetuate his memory by creating a monument named after him in the shape of a reserved forest where the dumb animals he loved so much may find a sanctuary and a haven of refuge, presided over by the benign spirit of the benefactor that made their preservation and their perpetuation in peace and happiness possible.

—R.R.M.'s review of *My India* in *Amrita Bazar Patrika*,
Calcutta, 17 April 1960

Deliverance for Rudraprayag

Reactions to the Slaying of the
Man-eating Leopard by Corbett

Congratulatory Telegrams and Letters

Gurney House, Naini Tal

2 May 1926

Your brother has killed leopard, almost certainly
man-eater, after sitting throughout eleven
consecutive nights in same tree for him.
Congratulations and thanks for whole Garhwal,
particularly from Ibbotson.

—Telegram to Margaret Corbett from Ibbotson,
Deputy Commissioner, Naini Tal

My dear Capt. Corbett,

Allow me to thank you and congratulate you from the bottom
of my heart for shooting the man-eating leopard who killed so

many innocent women and children in Upper Garhwal. We, the Garhwalies, will ever remember you as the killer of the greatest enemy of Garhwal. I know how difficult it was to shoot that most cunning and sly beast. Perhaps you will remember that I had a talk with you about this beast at Naini Tal in 1924. I asked you to write to me your willingness to go to Rudraprayag to shoot him under the conditions you thought most suitable for the expedition, and I handed over your letter to the Finance Member to utilize your services; but unfortunately, the then Deputy Commissioner of Garhwal did not accept your proposals, and took other means to get the leopard killed. But, finally, it is you who was able to save Garhwal from this beast. You must be very proud of the wonderful deed of yours, and you fully deserve the pride and honour which we gratefully associate with your name.

—Letter to Jim Corbett from Mukandi Lal, BA (Oxon),
Barrister-at-Law, Member Legislative Council,
Lansdowne, Garhwal, 9 May 1926

Dear Capt. Corbett,

I am desired to thank you on behalf of the Government of the United Provinces for the valuable public service you have rendered in destroying the Rudraprayag man-eating leopard. This animal has preyed on the Rudraprayag neighbourhood for over seven years and has killed no less than 125 human victims. You have, at considerable private inconvenience, spent many weeks in pursuit of this pest and have cheerfully borne much hardship and danger. You have earned the gratitude of the people of Garhwal, and the Governor in Council desires me to send you his sincere thanks and his congratulations on a fine achievement.

—Letter to Jim Corbett from G.B. Lambert, United Provinces
Government, D.O. No. 738-Z, Naini Tal, 17 May 1926

Dear Sir,

I have been directed by Colonel, His Highness the Maharaja Sahib Bahadur to convey to you His Highness' very best congratulations on your keen sportsmanship in putting an end to the notorious man-eating leopard. His Highness also wishes me to express his great delight at your being able to get rid of that terrible enemy and pest of the public of Garhwal. You have really done a great service not only to the people of Rudraprayag but to mankind in general.

With renewed congratulations and best of luck...

—Letter to Jim Corbett from the Private Secretary to H.H.
The Maharaja of Dhar, 19 May 1926

Reactions in the Press

Jim Corbett

Of all the daring deeds in the annals of shikar, there is, perhaps, nothing to beat the way in which Mr James Corbett has just again rid the district of a man-eating tigress which, during the past four or five months, had killed several natives within a couple of miles of Muktesar. Some of the bacteriological staff there had sat up, in vain, over the brute's kills without being able to get a shot, and had at last appealed to the Deputy Commissioner to make some arrangement for its destruction. On the news reaching Mr Corbett, he at once started off and, after a rough rainy night spent in the jungles, he tracked the tigress and sighted her, just as she was over her mid-day meal. Now was his chance; so he crept over some very rough ground covered with thorny brushwood and, coming within close firing distance, he had a difficult shot from his double-barrel rifle and missed. Before he had even time to replace the cartridge, the brute, infuriated at being disturbed, simply flung herself at her assailant, and their respective fates hung upon the single remaining cartridge in the rifle. But Mr Corbett awaited the rush with perfect coolness, and when the tigress was within about three yards, he bowled her over dead. Bravo, Sir!

—*The Lake Zephyr: A Social Weekly*, 21 April 1909

The Rudraprayag Man-Eater

The notorious man-eating leopard of Rudraprayag which, for seven years, had been the terror of a large and well-populated area of West Garhwal, has at last been killed. The sinister career of the animal, details of which appear on another page today, forms one of the most remarkable stories in the realms of truth or fiction. No less than 125 human victims have been directly traced to the brute; they have usually been pounced upon while in their houses at night and carried away into the jungle. The beast had had numerous wonderful escapes from both British and Indian shikaris who had, for long, been making strenuous efforts to put an end to the pest. The leopard appears to have thriven on poisoned kills, and displayed most astounding caution when traps of various kinds were laid for it. Twice it is recorded that the animal was actually captured by the people of the locality, on one occasion in a cave and on another in a trap; but each time it succeeded in getting away before it could be disposed of. It is little wonder that the Garhwalis had attributed to the beast supernatural powers for which no human agency was a match. Captain Corbett, of Naini Tal, who has had considerable experience of many kinds of shikar, spent ten strenuous weeks in tracking the animal before shooting it on the night of the 1st of May, and he underwent many hardships and risks during that time. Captain Corbett has refused to claim the Government reward of Rs 500, which had been offered for the disposal of the animal; but it is to be hoped that the successful accomplishment of the difficult task and his nota⁕ e service in freeing the people of West Garhwal from the terrible scourge will be suitably recognized. Captain Corbett received a great deal of assistance in tracking the leopard from Mr A.W. Ibbotson, the Deputy Commissioner of Garhwal. The latter journeyed to Rudraprayag as frequently as his duties would allow, and often was the companion of Captain Corbett in night watches over human kills and other eerie work involved.

Notorious Man-Eating Leopard Destroyed

The Fate of the Rudraprayag Pest

One Hundred and Twenty-Five Human Victims

(From a Naini Tal Correspondent)

The man-eating leopard, which has lately been widely known as the Rudraprayag pest and has, during the past seven years, killed 125 human beings in the western part of the Garhwal district, has at last been shot, having fallen to the rifle of Captain J. Corbett, of Gurney House, Naini Tal.

A Strange Story

The career of the animal makes one of the strangest of the many strange stories told of the Himalayas, so strange, indeed, that it might be doubted if the details, many of them tragic and gruesome, were not so well established. The first few instalments of the story were published in *The Pioneer* in December when the efforts of Mr X (who may now be identified as Captain Corbett) to bag the animal last autumn were described. The final chapter can now be written. The western part of Garhwal, in which the animal had committed its depredations, is comparatively well populated, and there are some 50,000 people in the area of some 350 square miles in which it roamed. Rudraprayag, from which the animal had been called, is a hamlet close to the borders of the Tehri State. It is at the junction of the Alaknanda river, which, when it reaches the plains at Hardwar, becomes the Ganges and the Mandakini rivers. Here, also, is the junction of the pilgrim routes to the holy shrines of Kedarnath and Badrinath. The area comprises a considerable amount of scrub jungle, and parts of it are honeycombed with caves formed by the waters of the Alaknanda cutting their way to the plains. Rudraprayag was the centre from which operations against the leopard were conducted. The leopard had been the terror of an area about 22 miles long and 18 miles broad on the east bank of the Alaknanda, and an area of about equal extent on the west bank.

A Regular Toll

It started killing human beings in 1918, and took a regular toll of the people of the affected area until it was finally disposed of on 1st of May. Its victims were generally snatched from inside houses or from the entrances to houses at night. It was particularly active during the summer months, when people desire to have their doors open at night. In recent years, the fear of the leopard has been such that, even in the stifling hot weather, houses have been closed up and barricaded at night. At least three pilgrims have been among the beast's victims during the past two years, but the pilgrims were usually avoided by the man-eater because they were, as a rule, in bands of considerable size and their shelters at night were well-protected by lights.

The Campaign against the Pest

In the previous articles in The Pioneer on the subject of the Rudraprayag pest, details were given of some of the many devices which were unsuccessfully resorted to in order to rid the area of the dreaded scourge. Sixteen shikaris paid by the Government had vainly endeavoured to dispose of the animal. Gun licenses had been freely issued in the district, and the Government had supplied specially constructed traps as well as poison in the hopes of ending the beast's career. The leopard had been caught twice, once in a trap and once in a cave, but it had got away on each occasion, while the frightened people on the spot were sending miles away across the hills for specially chosen men they hoped would shoot it. As there is an inclination in certain quarters to blame the Government for all the evils from which India suffers, the Government had been blamed for permitting the existence of the Rudraprayag leopard. The Government had done what they could in the matter, and had spent altogether Rs 1,518 on the measures already described.Legislative Councillors, who had been inclined to be indignant at the Government's inability to rid Garhwal of its scourge, had ignored the invitation given to go to Rudraprayag themselves to try and lay the animal low. Less talkative people had on various occasions essayed the task.

Some three years ago two military officers made an effort, and Captain Corbett, who has had considerable experience of various kinds of shikar, concentrated on the task for a whole month, from the 16th of September to the 16th of October, last year. He was ably and enthusiastically assisted by Mr A.W. Ibbotson, the Deputy Commissioner of Garhwal, who spent on the work as much time as he could spare from his official duties. But as already recorded, the animal was so extraordinarily cautious that gun traps, gin traps, the most careful tracking, the sitting up over human kills, the poisoning of the kills with strychnine, arsenic, and cyanide were of no avail. The uncanny wariness displayed by the animal on many occasions, its ability to sense when there was danger about, and its various wonderful escapes had led the simple inhabitants of those parts to the conclusion that the man-eater had supernatural powers; they believed the brute was possessed of an evil spirit which no human agency could exercise.

Operations Resumed

It has already been explained that it was considered advisable, after the 16th of October, to leave the animal alone for a few months as the more it was harried the warier it became and, during the winter, its human victims were not generally numerous. This plan was adopted, and it was not until the 16th of March last that Mr Ibbotson and Captain Corbett returned to the little rest house at Rudraprayag and re-opened their campaign against the man-eater. In the meantime, they had been carrying out experiments with patent machans, gun traps, and flash lights. When they arrived at Rudraprayag, the bridges over the river were closed at night, and various other precautions were taken. The man-eater had been busy this year before the 16th of March. He started killing human beings again in January and, between then and the 16th of March, eight victims had been added to his previous total of 114. From the 16th of March until the 1st of May, Captain Corbett was continually on the animal's tracks, and he was again assisted by Mr Ibbotson who was always in the neighbourhood of Rudraprayag when his duties permitted.

The frightful activities of the man-eater continued. On the night of the 1st of April, the animal snatched a man from inside a house. At dawn on the 7th of April, an old woman of 85 in a village two and a half miles from Rudraprayag was seized near her house which she had just left, and was carried half a mile away. A boy of fifteen at a village 18 miles due east of Rudraprayag was the next victim, on the 14th of April.

Narrow Escapes

Meantime, Mr Ibbotson and Captain Corbett had also been active. Part of the body of the man killed on the 1st of April was poisoned. The leopard returned to the kill and ate a part of the body which was not poisoned. On the 3rd, it ate a part of the body which had been treated with poison but seemed to suffer no ill effects. After the kill on the 7th of April, two ingenious traps were set. Two rifles with the muzzles directed on the kill were secured to a tree; lines of fishing tackle joined their triggers to the kill. It had been hoped that the leopard would pull the lines and, thus, let off the rifles when it returned to the kill on the night of the 8th. It was thought probable that it would endeavour to move the kill away from the rifles in the same direction that it had carried its victim on the previous night. With the object of ensuring that it should do this, a number of bushes were stuck in the ground near the kill, between the kill and the rifles. The leopard came at 7.45 p.m. on the 8th, pulled up the bushes, dropped them down a *khud*, and then moved the kill in the direction of the rifles. The fishing lines were thus slackened and the rifles did not go off. The animal was disturbed, and, in springing away, landed on a huge gin trap some six feet or seven feet in length, which had been hidden nearby. Mr Ibbotson and Captain Corbett who were in the nearest tree—the leopard usually conveyed its victims to a spot where there were no trees within easy range—about 100 yards away, immediately rushed to the trap. There was no animal in the trap but a tuft of hair was sticking in its jaws.

Eleven Nights' Sitting Up

On the 20th of April, Captain Corbett decided that he would sit up for the leopard for at least ten nights near Golabrai *chatti*, a grass shelter for pilgrims, half a mile from the Rudraprayag rest house on the pilgrim road. Between the 10th and 20th of April, the pug marks of the leopard had been seen near this chatti, where last year it had killed three people. Captain Corbett believed there was a probability of it appearing there again, at any rate once, during the following ten nights. He sat up in a machan in a tree by the chatti and above the road. On the road below, he had a goat secured with a bell round its neck. Captain Corbett sat up for ten nights on this machan, without seeing or hearing any signs of the leopard. He then thought it would be well to persevere in sitting up for one more night, that of the 1st of May, and he did so. The man-eater was due to kill that night. For days earlier, the animal had had what was believed to have been his last feed, this being from a goat which had been taken from a house. On the last day of April, the beast had made an unsuccessful attempt to secure a human kill.

A Lucky Shot

It was at 10 p.m. on the 1st of May that Captain Corbett heard from his machan something rush down the road, and the bell on the goat tinkle. Captain Corbett looked down on the road and saw an indistinct blur in the direction of which he pointed his rifle. He switched on his electric torch and found that the bead of his rifle was drawn on the body of a leopard and fired. The leopard made a spring and disappeared. All this happened in little more than a second, and the leopard got away so quickly that had Captain Corbett not very luckily found, when he switched on the light, that he was already covering the leopard with his rifle, he would have had no opportunity of adjusting his aim before the leopard leapt away. Captain Corbett spent a very anxious night, not knowing whether he had killed the leopard or not. The moon, which appeared at 3 o'clock in the morning, did not reveal any signs of it. At daybreak, Captain Corbett set out to look for the animal. He found blood tracks which led to the leopard, lying dead in a hole into which it had fallen fifty yards down the khud. It may be mentioned that 100 pilgrims had spent the night in the Golabrai chatti.

Identifying the Man-Eater

There are sufficient good reasons for identifying this leopard with the man-eater. In all the human kills by the Rudraprayag leopard, there have been three teeth marks showing that the leopard was one short of its full complement of teeth. The leopard shot by Captain Corbett had one tooth broken. The man-eater had been shot at three years ago by the military officers already referred to, and had left behind, on that occasion, smears of blood which indicated that it had been hit in the foot. The leopard of Captain Corbett had the mark of an old bullet wound in the foot. Moreover, a piece of hair was missing from its right hind leg where there was apparently a recently healed scar; this evidently corresponded with the tuft of hair found in the trap on the 8th of April. About the animal's body were a number of old scars and some more recent ones. Two weeks before its death, Captain Corbett had heard two leopards fighting. This suggests how the man-eater had received its scars. In various ways, the leopard, in appearance, fulfilled the generally accepted theories concerning man-eaters. It was a light-coloured and evidently very old animal, with an indifferent coat and practically no whiskers. Its length was 7 feet 10 inches, an exceptional size, particularly for a hill leopard. This measurement was taken after it had been lying in a hole all night in which it had probably shrunk to some extent.

The People's Gratitude

News of the shooting spread rapidly in the affected area and hundreds of people from neighbouring hamlets went to see the body as it lay in the Rudraprayag rest house on 1st of May. Upon catching sight of it and noticing some of the peculiar details mentioned in the description of the beast, they were unanimous in declaring it to be the *adam khoar* (man-eater), and expressed delight at being at last rid of their terrible enemy and great gratitude to Mr Ibbotson and Corbett for persevering until completion of what had seemed to them a superhuman task.

If the courage and determination displayed by Mr Ibbotson and Captain Corbett in their relentless pursuit of the man-eater had not been of an exceptional order, the people would still be wondering whose turn it was next to be carried away and suffer a horrible death.

It should be explained that Captain Corbett has had no interest in the matter beyond keen sportsmanship and to free the people of Garhwal from their pest and he has refused to claim the Rs 500 which the Government had offered for the destruction of the man-eater. He expects shortly to proceed to East Africa where he has a coffee estate. He delayed his journey there much longer than he originally intended, in the hope, which has now been fulfilled, of defeating the wily man-eater. Captain Corbett reckons him a poor shikari who cannot get the better of any average leopard in four days. Sufficient has been said to prove that the Rudraprayag pest was possessed of intelligence which is fortunately above that of the average leopard, and why the bringing of it to bag cost over ten weeks' hard work.

—*The Pioneer*, Saturday, 15 May 1926

Corbett's Influence

The Man-Eaters of Kumaon and the Chhindwara Court Case

Craft of Man-Eaters in C.P.*

Chhindwara Court Rejects Murder Theory

(By Our Special Correspondent)

NAGPUR, TUESDAY: In connection with the menace of man-eaters in the villages of C.P. comes an interesting story from Chhindwara: of how the crafty animal not only catches its prey unawares but also throws dust in the eyes of the police sometimes.

Was the victim killed by a man-eater or murdered by the accused produced by the prosecution was the question that came up before the District and Sessions Judge, Chhindwara. The verdict went

---

* Central Provinces.

against the Police, and the man-eater that has been ravaging the villages near Chhindwara was adjudged the killer.

Jim Corbett's *Man-Eaters of Kumaon* was produced in court, and extracts from it read out by the counsel for defence in a recent murder case in a Chhindwara Sessions Court.

The prosecution story was that Smt. Biria, wife of Todal, Raghubhar and Bansi had conspired to bring about the murder of one Todal who was found dead in the jungle on 19 September 1949. The police theory was that Biria and Raghubhar were in love with each other, and enlisted the help of their friend Bansi to get rid of Todal. The defence theory was that it was a man-eating tiger that killed Todal.

In support of their defence, the accused produced copies of the *C.P. and Berar Gazette* which announced rewards for killing man-eating tigers who were playing havoc with men and cattle. The depredations caused by these wild animals were admitted to be frequent.

Passages from Corbett Cited

The counsel for defence read out the following passage from Jim Corbett's *Man-Eaters of Kumaon* to suggest a surprise attack on Todal by a man-eater: 'Tigers do not know that human beings have no sense of smell, and when a tiger becomes a man-eater, it treats human beings exactly as it treats a wild animal, that is, it approaches its victims up-wind or lies up in wait for them down-wind. The significance of this will be apparent when it is realized that while the sportsman is trying to get a sight of the tiger, the tiger in all probability is trying to stalk the sportsman lying up in wait for him. The contest owing to the tiger's height, colouring, and ability to move without making a sound would be very unequal were it not for the wind factor operating in favour of the sportsman. In all cases where killing is done by stalking or stealth, the victim is approached from behind.'

The doctor who conducted the post-mortem, which could be done only after four days of death, could not say whether the death was due to Todal being mauled by a man-eater, but he could not deny that the injury could not be caused by the teeth of a tiger. Here again, they had to fall back upon Jim Corbett who has given an account of his dressing up a girl badly mauled by a tiger, and the wounds described there are almost like the wounds on Todal's body.

The assessors, in this case, were of the opinion that it was a case of depredation by a man-eater.

Acquitting the accused, Shri M.L. Shrivastava, Sessions Judge, Chhindwara, observes: 'The police has missed the relevant clues and worked on the clue of possible motive to build up an edifice which failed to get support from facts. The presence of a man-eater in the jungle which was creating a ravage in the locality was not considered at all. In the jungles, besides perils from man there are perils from wild beasts.'

—From Vol. XVIII, No. 163, *The Nagpur Times*,
15 June 1949.

Dear Hawkins,

… I wonder if you saw a report in *The Nagpur Times* of a murder trial at Chhindwara during which *Man-eaters* figured. I believe that this is the first time that a book, other than a legal one, has been produced in a court of law, and accepted as evidence. Let me know if you have not seen the report and I will send you a copy. If properly handled in America, the report would do *Man-eaters* and our other books a lot of good, for it would show the people of America the reliance the people of India place on our publications. It is for this reason that I am so anxious that *My India* should be up to the standard you set for *Man-eaters*...

—Jim Corbett's letter to Roy E. Hawkins from
Nyeri, Kenya, 22 October 1949

Epigraph

[Jim Corbett penned his final book on 6 April 1955, and thirteen days later he died after a massive heart attack. He was buried the next day at the St Peter's Anglican Church cemetery. He was nearing eighty. Throughout his life, Corbett was very keen on helping the poor people. After his death, Corbett's estate was divided and a bulk of it given to the poor folks. A strip of land that he had bought was divided into several plots, homes were built on them, and these were given to the homeless. He had a stone wall built surrounding the village of Choti Haldwani to protect the crops from marauding animals. He also provided food, medicine, and money to those who needed them. He listened to the problems of villagers and found remedies for them. The people in Kumaon still regard him as a saint. There has been no other white man who has done so much for the people of Kumaon with the exception of Sir Henry Ramsay. Part of the royalty from his books still goes to St Dunstan's fund for the blind; the rest goes to his blind nephew, George Marshall. Eight years after Jim's death, his sister Maggie died, on Boxing Day, 26 December 1963. She was cremated and the ashes were interred in Jim's grave.—Editor]

It is a far cry from Nyeri in Kenya, where Jim Corbett recently died, to Kaladhungi in Naini Tal where he grew up, roaming the forests both as boy and man, absorbing the jungle lore which enabled him to emerge unscathed from quests of the most dreaded man-eating tigers and leopards that have ever been known in northern India.

To hunt tigers, and especially the man-eating variety, alone on foot, calls for a degree of courage that is given to few; yet Colonel Corbett was big enough to admit that the proximity of a tiger always left him 'breathless'.

But, though his fame is generally linked with the hunting of tigers, it is clear from his books that this passion was rivalled by his benevolence for those whom he called 'the poor of India'. He recently donated the money for a *panchayat-ghar* to be erected in Kaladhungi, and he has for decades paid the land revenue of his 'tenants'.

It is a pity that his house has been left unattended; it could perhaps be renovated and used as a showpiece for tourists.

As the news travels through the hills and mountains—Corbett Sahib is dead—those who have known this fabulous hunter and humanitarian will pause at a temple and hillside shrine to offer a prayer. Home is the hunter.

—'New Delhi Notebook', *The Statesman*, New Delhi,
26 April 1955